The Sonoma Map Key

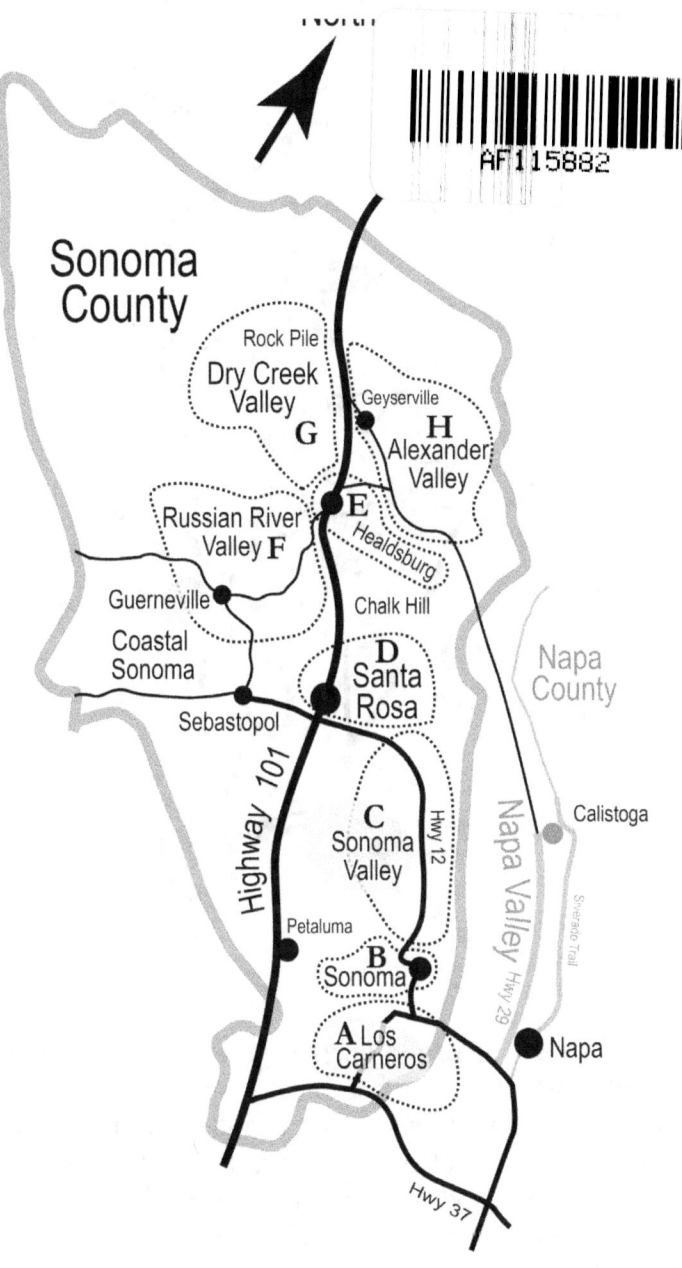

The Dotted Circles describe the general coverage of the maps but they often overlap. Some zones have multiple maps that split the areas into east and west, with detailed maps of the nearest downtowns. These are not based on the borders of the American Viticulture Areas but are arranged for ease of navigation.

Main Winery Areas

Sonoma is a place of great beauty, mystery and fertility, and her most remarkable feature is her diversity. She is like a beautiful woman with many skills and talents, yet she still tends the garden, prepares the food and sings the songs of her ancestors. When you are standing on the banks of the Russian River, surrounded by a fairy ring of giant redwood trees stretching from deep in the earth up to the heavens, it is reassuring to realize that there is that much beauty in the world. When you breathe in the salt spray of the rolling Pacific Ocean, standing on the spectacular Sonoma coastline, it is inspiring. When you sit on a patio sipping a glass of wine in one

Around the City of Sonoma

of Sonoma's abundantly fertile valleys, enjoying the view of the vines, it is intoxicating on more than just the physical level. When you visit Sonoma, you are experiencing the deep beauty of the divine feminine, so it's no wonder that it feels so special!

About Convenient Los Carneros

At the southern edge of the two counties is a thin slice of land at the top of the San Pablo Bay, called Los Carneros. Its wind-whipped, basaltic, highly drained vineyards are planted like a carpet with Pinot Noir and Chardonnay, in a continuous swath of precise

Sonoma & Napa Los Carneros

green lines. nd well worth the visit for their bright and refreshing wines. The fact that it is so convenient to San Francisco makes it a popular daytrip destination. Many of the first 'Carneros' wineries you encounter in Sonoma coming north see hordes of visitors, so they price their wines accordingly. But when you go a little ways off the beaten path you will find numerous premium producers.

Sonoma Winery Maps
280 Winery Directory, Touring & Tasting Tips

Contents

The Map Key   3
Main Winery Areas - Map - 4
Around the City of Sonoma - Map A - 5
Sonoma & Napa Los Carneros - Map B - 10
The Sonoma Plaza - Notes - Map C - 7
The Sonoma Valley - Notes - Map D - 10
Glen Ellen - Map E - 11
Around Santa Rosa - Map - 12
Hwy 101 and Downtown Santa Rosa - Map - 13
Downtown Healdsburg - Map F - 14
Notes: Northern Sonoma & Healdsburg   15
Russian River Valley Overview - Map - 16
The Russian River Valley - Notes - Map G - 17
North of River Rd - Westside Ave - Map H - 18
South of River Rd - Notes - Map I - 19
Dry Creek Valley Overview - Map - 20
The Dry Creek Valley - Notes - Map J - 21
The Southern Dry Creek Valley - Map K - 22
The Northern Dry Creek Valley - Map L - 23
Alexander Valley Overview - Notes - Map - 24
Alexander Valley - Map M - 25
Southern Alexander Valley - Map N - 26
Northern Alexander Valley - Map O - 27
Bay Area Main Roads - Map - 28
Sonoma AVA Dates - Map - 34
Popular Routes - Map 40

Chapters

Chapter 1: Creating a Daytrip Strategy - 29
Chapter 2: Getting Around Sonoma - 35
Chapter 3: The ABC's of Wine Tasting - 41
Chapter 4: Winery Directory - 43
Other Titles by the Authors - 111
About - 112

Sonoma Winery Maps
280 Winery Directory,
Touring & Tasting Tips
Ralph & Lahni DeAmicis
Authors of the Dream Tour Series

Published by
Cuore Libre Publishing
Napa, California

To Order Copies visit
www.AmicisTours.com

Copyright © 2013, 2014, 2022, 2023, 2024, 2025
by Ralph & Lahni DeAmicis
Photos: Lahni DeAmicis
Maps: Ralph DeAmicis
Versions of these maps have appeared in previous editions our tour books beginning in 2007.
Maps Updated 6/1/2024
ISBN 979-8-3492-0181-3

Disclaimer: We create these books through extensive research that includes having visited many of these wineries multiple times. But we make no guarantees for the accuracy of the information included herein, and accept no responsibility for any losses or inconvenience you may suffer from using this product. Important: Our advice is intended to help you stay safe while you enjoy the region, but mixing alcohol and driving is a risky endeavor. We suggest that you approach it cautiously by having a designated or professional driver. We want you to have a fun time in Wine Country and come back and visit again and again.

Ralph & Lahni DeAmicis

Sonoma Plaza

Sonoma Plaza

The valley and the town of Sonoma are economically linked to the world by the Sonoma Highway (Hwy 12), because unlike Napa, there is no river to promote commerce. The Plaza, and its surrounding streets, are California's most historic location because it is the home of California's twenty-first and final *Franciscan Mission*, the Spanish military barracks, and the site of the *Bear Flag Rebellion* monument.

To the east of the Plaza, next to the **Sebastiani** Winery, is the 'Town Vineyard', where the missionaries first planted vines in the 1820's. Further east is **California's first modern winery, Buena Vista**, established in the mid-1800's, and nearby is their contemporary, **Gundlach Bundschu**.

Sprinkled around California's largest Plaza is a wonderful collection of restaurants, shops, galleries and of course, tasting rooms.

On the Plaza are *picnic grounds and a Visitor Center* in an old Carnegie Library. The layout of the paseos (passageways) and courtyards with their stucco and ceramic tiles gives the town the feeling of what it once was, a Mexican Pueblo at the northern tip of the Spanish empire.

Sonoma Valley

The Sonoma Valley has been farmed by the same families for generations, so it has that comfy confidence that comes from knowing who they are and where they belong. Its popularity is helped by being an incredibly convenient destination from much of the Bay Area. The town of Sonoma sits in the southern third of the Valley, with wineries in all directions, but the largest concentration starts five miles north of the Sonoma Plaza on Highway 12, beginning at the Madrone Road traffic light. There are four wineries near this intersection, **Abbot's Passage (site of the historic Valley of the Moon Winery), B.R. Cohn Winery, Little Family, and Hamel Family.** Around the next curve is Imagery, which produces small lots of unusual wines and has a unique, curated wine label art program. They share a driveway with low Arrowood.

Further north just off Highway 12, on Dunbar Road are three small, unique wineries. **Loxton Cellars**, where you walk past the press and tanks to get to the bar, and where you can taste with the winemaker. Next door is **Wellington Cellars** and down the street is **Lasseter Family**, owned by the head of Pixar. Further north are the caves at **Deerfield Ranch**, and across the road you will see the expansive vineyards of the **Kunde Family**. Next up are the widely distributed **Kenwood and Chateau Saint Jean** (pronounced 'Jeen') Wineries, both of which sit beyond their vineyards. Across from St Jean is **Saint Anne's Crossing**, a popular stop for the Zinfandel lovers.

For the visitor, **one of the most important is VJB Vineyard**, because it makes an idyllic spot to taste their wines outdoors in an Italian-style Piazza with a delicious lunch from their deli, outdoor barbecue or pizza ovens! Wellington Cellars is their 'sister winery'. As you head farther north, at the next corner is **Landmark Vineyards** with their beautiful gardens, started by members of the John Deere family but since sold to new owners. Down that road is the diminutive **La Rochelle Winery** tasting room with their lovely garden. Coincidentally, both wineries specialize in excellent Pinot Noir and Chardonnay.

At the top of the valley at a rare traffic light is the **Saint Francis Winery,** with its charming California mission-style building and stunning views of Sugar Loaf Mountain and Mount Hood. Just past there is the **Ledson Winery**, a dramatic looking building and popular wedding venue.

For lunch or dinner there are numerous restaurants in downtown Sonoma, Glen Ellen and Kenwood, as well as store front tasting rooms and markets. Tucked up in the hills are more wineries that are open by appointment. If you plan to picnic, we suggest buying your supplies early and keeping it in a cooler, because the lunchtime lines can be long and slow. You can't bring food to any venue that serves their own.

If you want to have an early dinner, which is always a good idea on a wine touring day, downtown Sonoma is a great place for that. Here, farm to table is the norm, not the exception.

The 'Wine Country Casual' dress code applies in the restaurants, so generally the style that you wore to go wine tasting works fine for dinner at all but the fanciest restaurants. More importantly, bring something warmer to wear in the evening because once the sun begins to set, it cools down quickly even on the hottest day.

The Sonoma Valley
'Valley of the Moon'

Breakfast

Before a tour, always have a good breakfast that includes protein and fat. Adding a little toast is okay but avoid high carb meals like pancakes with syrup and fruit. It is helpful to understand that alcohol is post-digested sugar so adding sweets to that can make you 'loopy' pretty quickly.

Sonoma Valley
Glen Ellen

Water

Hydration is very important because alcohol is dehydrating. Bring two to three bottles of cold water for each person in the car to drink between wineries. One of Ralph's most repeated phrases is, "The secret to a good wine tour is how much water you drink!" Normally consume one ounce of water for each ounce of wine. On hot days it is common for the humidity levels to be twenty to thirty percent, so people lose significant moisture through their skin. On those days you may need to drink up to two ounces of water for each ounce of wine consumed.

Around Santa Rosa

Lunch

Plan your lunch before you go out the door and choose a location within fifteen minutes of the wineries. If you're picnicking at a winery (many don't permit that, so check), get your lunch supplies on the way to your first stop to avoid the lunchtime rush at the markets. If you're going to a restaurant, make a reservation. By the way, those breadsticks at the wineries are not meant as food. Their purpose is to scrub the young tannins off your tongue, so the wines don't all taste the same. If you are doing a food pairing, don't expect that to replace a meal. Due to local regulations, those portions will be small.

HIghway 101 & Downtown Santa Rosa

Dinner

Wine tasting is hard work. It combines socializing, travel, walking and intense sensory experiences far beyond what you normally experience. You will be tired. Our suggestion is to plan your meal before the tour, place your order early and pick it up on the way back and have it on your patio. We've lost count of the number of guests who blew off dinner reservations at fine restaurants after a wine tour because they fell asleep. If you really want to eat out, plan an early casual dinner immediately after the last winery, near your hotel.

Downtown Healdsburg

Notes: Northern Sonoma & Healdsburg

Not many years ago, Healdsburg was a quiet farming town that served an important support role for the many farmers in the three nearby growing regions, Russian River, Dry Creek and Alexander Valleys. That changed in the 1970's when northern California winemakers shifted away from making cheap jug wines in favor of premium varietals, which attracted tourists. Because nearby Santa Rosa is the primary commercial hub, the smaller, countrified Healdsburg was ripe for a tourism upgrade.

The transformation was less extreme than Napa Valley's Yountville, where private homes and run-down bars, gave way to new hotels and restaurants. Healdsburg held onto more of their history and personality, and the result is a charming plaza surrounded by a mix of old and new.

Besides attracting a steady stream of tourists, the changes also attracted new prosperous residents. If Healdsburg were as close to San Francisco as downtown Sonoma, it would be as busy, but the two-hour drive on Highway 101 to the downtown exit filters out the less serious enthusiasts. Healdsburg led the way in encouraging storefront tasting rooms. Many local towns discouraged them, deciding that those activities should stay in the valleys.

They didn't want the competition for the bars and restaurants, and they didn't want drunken tourists staggering down their streets. But Healdsburg dealt with a special circumstance. The nearby wineries are predominantly small, family affairs situated on narrow, winding, heavily forested roads, with neighbors who like their quiet surroundings. The expense of converting farm buildings into legal tasting rooms can be prohibitive, and their neighbor's objections can stall their projects for years.

Downtown tasting rooms have proven an economical alternative and they have become an important part of the scene! The amazing diversity of varietals grown locally allows tasting rooms to establish unique niches. The result is a remarkably wide selection of varietals available to taste, all within

Russian River Valley Overview

strolling distance of each other. Healdsburg has good hotels, bed and breakfasts, inns, and a wonderful restaurant scene, plus plenty of upscale shopping. Like most of the Wine Country towns, as compared to many tourist areas, it has a large full-time population, because the wineries are big employers. While there are houses that tourists can rent, most Wine Country towns strictly regulate that, so the selection is small.

Russian River Valley

The Russian River Valley

This region is named for the river that flows south through the Alexander Valley, the Dry Creek Valley and then turns west in the Russian River Valley, on the way to the Pacific Ocean. Imperial Russia established a settlement on the coast in the 1800's to grow food for their settlements in Alaska. Eventually, their 'Fort Ross', or 'Rossiya', named for Mother Russia, became the base for a profitable fur trade. Their settlement attracted other Eastern Europeans, including the **Korbel** brothers, whose winery continues making popular sparkling wines in Guerneville. Sparkling wines are generally made from Chardonnay and Pinot Noir grapes and those varietals thrive in the bright sunshine and cool climate that the Pacific Coast happily provides.

East Russian River Valley - North of River Road - Westside Road

Notes: Westside Road

The popular stretch of road immediately south of downtown Healdsburg is home to a shockingly large number of high-quality wineries located near to each other. Being on the climatic line between the Dry Creek and Russian River Valleys you can find a wider variety of wines than in most areas.

Russian River Valley - South of River Road & North of Highway 12

Notes: Olivet Road

A cool group of about ten wineries sits on the rolling hills around the short and very straight Olivet Road, which runs from River Road in the north to Guerneville Road in the south. This area is known for its high-water table and gently rolling hills. These are all small wineries, mostly family owned. While the featured grapes are Pinot Noir and Chardonnay, there are numerous old Zinfandel vines here and there. The collection of wineries there include Harvest Moon, DeLoach, Benovia, Inman, Pellegrini, and Battaglini.

Dry Creek Valley Overview

Downtown
Map G5

The Dry Creek Valley

The Dry Creek Valley is a small, almond shaped slice of heaven aligned from northwest to southeast, with Lake Sonoma at the top, the 'Dry' Creek in the center and the Russian River at the bottom. The valley sits to the west of downtown Healdsburg, but most of the wineries are located to the northwest.

Dry Creek Valley

See K for the South Half

See L for the North Half

Southern Dry Creek Valley

A Creek Runs Down the Center

It has two north-south roads on either side of the creek. Dry Creek Road starts north of downtown at Healdsburg Avenue. It also intersects Highway 101. It is a relatively straight road and most of the wineries are along its length. The road changes names near the Lake Sonoma Dam, where it turns west and heads towards the Pacific and becomes the amazingly winding Skaggs Creek Road.

Northern Dry Creek Valley

Parallel to Dry Creek Road, on the other side of the creek, is West Dry Creek Road. That starts at the southern edge of downtown Healdsburg, on the other (west) side of Highway 101, coming off Westside Road. It travels north the length of the valley, ending just below Lake Sonoma. Its path is narrow and twisted so avoid it unless you are going to a specific winery.

Alexander Valley Overview

Notes: Alexander Valley

Alexander Valley is the easiest of the three valleys to navigate because Highway 101 travels its length, with convenient exits at the important spots and it is paralleled by straight local roads. The quickest way between these spread-out wineries is often on '101'. The southeastern part of Alexander Valley Road (Highway 128) is home to a line of wineries; scenic **Hanna Vineyards, Silver Oak's environmentally efficient,** state of the art facility, **Alexander Valley Vineyards,** and the **Stonestreet** Winery, that sits, like a monolith on a bare rise. Stonestreet is the (Kendall) Jackson family's premium estate, where they use grapes from the northeastern hillsides across the

Alexander Valley

See N for the South Half

See O for the North Half

road. When Highway 128 heads north to Geyserville, Alexander Valley Road continues west to Healdsburg Avenue, passing the entrance to the **Jordan** Vineyards. Farther north, on the west side of the valley alongside Highway 101, are three large wineries; **Francis Ford Coppola** (their restaurant, Rustic, is the only place to eat in the valley), Clos Du Bois Winery (closed) and **Trione**. Landmark: The large white structure on the eastern hillside is the River Rock Casino parking garage. Two important factors shape the

Southern Alexander Valley

valley's flavors. They are the northeast to southwest orientation of the valley that aligns it with the setting sun, and the low western hills, that allow the strong afternoon sunshine to bake the valley floor vines. That bleaching sunlight forces the Merlot to produce more tannins, making the wines more structured. Meanwhile, the Cabernet is grown on the valley floor on forgiving gravel rather than rocky hillsides, so it produces somewhat softer wines. A muscular Merlot and an approachable Cabernet is the opposite of what most Cab lovers expect, but they are a tasty find. The classic style Cabernets, earthy, deep and needing time to age, more often come from the rocky hillsides, where the vines struggle to produce small, richly flavored grapes.   most Cab lovers expect, but they are a tasty find. The classic style Cabernets, earthy, deep and needing time to age, more often come from the

Northern Alexander Valley

rocky hillsides, where the vines struggle to produce small, richly flavored grapes. Thanks to the diversity of these three valleys, the Healdsburg area has become an important California wine center. The rising popularity of Pinot Noir accelerated their success. Only its greater distance from San Francisco protects it from being overwhelmed by visitors. While the casual tourist staying in San Francisco tends to visit the more convenient wineries to the south, the enthusiasts make the effort to drive a little farther to this gem of an area. Many repeat visitors live in the Bay Area and they appreciate the region's wide selection of wines and experiences that are casual, enriching, and affordable.

The Bay Area Main Roads

Chapter One:
Creating a Day Trip Strategy

Every wine tour needs a great strategy to take the best advantage of the day. Over the course of thousands of tours with clients, we've had the opportunity to see what works, and what doesn't. Here are some of our best tips! The first step is to start early! If drinking wine in the morning seems excessive, remember, you are in a 'tasting' room, not a 'drinking' room. You are there to evaluate and enjoy the wines, not aiming to get a buzz on. There is a big difference between wine tasting and bar hopping!

Winery tasting rooms are generally open from 10am to 5pm. So, if you arrive early the staff is still fresh. Many people working in the tasting rooms routinely taste each bottle to make sure the wine is okay, and the alcohol adds up. By the latter part of the day, they can get pretty loose, and by the end of the day they are also tired. You want them pouring for you when they are sharp and happy to answer questions.

Also, if it is an open tasting room with other clients around, it can get noisy and a little messy later in the day, and the service can be a bit iffy. The best times to taste are between 10am and 3pm. That doesn't mean people don't frequently go to 5pm and bit more, if they can manage it. For the wineries, sometimes those late day tastings, when guests are feeling no pain, can be good sales opportunities. But, from your side of the tasting bar, if you want to avoid buying more wine than you intended, avoid stretching the day.

As tour drivers, we believe strongly in the good sense of hiring someone to drive for you, rather than taking the chance of drinking and driving with the inherent physical and legal risks that entails. However, we know from experience that many people drive themselves, and if care and moderation are taken, it can be done safely. We explain how to do that in the next chapter. Also, even when you hire a driver, you may want to plan the tour yourself, especially if the person driving is not an expert on the wine region.

Transportation is the largest employer of men in America, so you can figure that a certain percentage live by their GPS and are clueless about the winding, steep canyon roads that make up wine country.

Local tour guides rarely depend on GPS because the limited number of towers combined with the steep hills makes it undependable. When you plan your day the first question is whether or not you are driving yourself, because those suggest two differnt strategies.

When driving yourself, plan the longest leg of the trip for the beginning of the day, when you have no alcohol in your system. Head to the farthest winery first, and then plan that each subsequent leg of the trip will bring you closer to your starting point. Plan to have lunch after the first winery at a location on the route between the first and the second winery. Don't rush lunch, but do not let it take more than an hour. When driving yourself visiting two wineries, one before and one after a gracious lunch, is the max. For the winery after lunch, choose one that is as close to where you are staying as possible.

That doesn't mean it needs to be next to your hotel, although if there was a spectacular tasting room walking distance, that would be fine. In fact, some of the downtown wineries these days are excellent for walk-about tastings. In any case your ride back from the final winery, when you are tired and maybe a little tipsy, shouldn't be more than about ten to fifteen minutes. Two wineries in a day with a lunch in between is safe, if the person driving exercises moderation, eats plenty of protein and fat and drinks enough water: one ounce for each ounce of wine.

If someone is driving who is not drinking, you can plan a little differently and visit more wineries. The first winery will be closer to your starting point. Choose a winery where the wines will be light in flavor and alcohol, so your palate can warm up and not become immediately saturated. With a designated driver you can go to two wineries before lunch.

The second winery should be the farthest from your starting point. That way you are relaxed by the wine and in a good mood for the ride between the first and the second winery. The next should feature 'bigger wines', with fuller flavors, which means fewer white wines and more reds (unless you don't like red wine). After the second tasting, enjoy a nice lunch, once again, high in protein and fat and low in simple carbohydrates.

Warning!!!

Never go to more than two tastings without eating! Often after the second winery you are feeling like you have superpowers, and you are up for another tasting adventure. Don't fall for that! If you do not get enough protein and fat into your system, your blood sugar will plummet, and you'll need a nap.

After lunch, the next winery should be closer to your starting point. Some tours lend themselves to a fourth winery. It depends on the types of wines you're drinking. The bigger, more expensive wines have higher alcohol and require longer tastings to allow them to open. The sparkling wines, whites and light reds are shorter sessions.

If you add a fourth winery it should be the closet to your starting point. What you want to avoid is a long drive back to your lodging when you are tired. At the end of the day, after a bunch of wine and sun, you will need a nap. The question is, do you want to take that nap in the car or beside the pool?

Hint: About that fourth winery. Having big red wines on top of big reds can so saturate the palate that it is hard to tell them apart, so having a prestigious red wine late in the day is often a waste of time and tasting endurance. Ideally, plan to visit those wineries immediately before and after lunch.

At the first winery your palate is still waking up and by the fourth winery your palate is saturated, and your nervous system is sedated, so it's hard to enjoy the flavors. The best wines for late in the day are sparkling wines, because their high acid levels and of course, the bubbles, clean the palate and bring a touch of delight and celebration to the end of the day.

Wineries have increasingly moved to seated tastings that require 90 minutes. Allow for 20 minutes between each stop and an hour for lunch, so three wineries take 5 to 7 hours and four wineries take 7 to 8 hours. When there were more 30-45 minute walk-in bar tastings, we could bring our guests to 5 wineries in 6 to 7 hours, but those are less common today.

It is a Matter of Timing

Early in the day, the staff tends to pour smaller samples, but as the day goes on the samples expand a bit so after 3pm, all bets are off, and you'd better watch out. As the day passes it is increasingly important to drink enough water. Late in the day most people forget. As a guide, I am continually handing guests cold bottles of spring water.

If the tasting room host knows you have a professional driver, they will often pour more wine because they're not concerned about you driving into a ditch. They will also pour better wines because they know that 'buyers' often hire drivers.

This is important because the winery staff works by commission and they know that the more wine they pour the more they sell. They pour more during the seated tastings, which give guests enough time to appreciate the wines and engage with the host, which is a big part of sales.

Not surprisingly, seated tasting sales are significantly higher than those at a bar, which is why bar tastings are disappearing. Wineries are good places to buy wine because they keep their best bottles for their visitors.

Watch out, occasionally hosts get out of control and take those big pours to extremes. First, that's dangerous because drunks get behind the wheel, or fall on their face. Second, excessive alcohol is toxic, and the guests suffer the next day.

Finally, inhibitions dissolve and visitors can find a nasty charge on their credit card bill, for wines they barely remember tasting or buying! That is why we suggest not stretching the day! It is also why we recommend using the 'dump buckets'.

Sonoma American Viticulture Area Dates

Alexander Valley, 1984
Bennett Valley, 2003
Carneros - Sonoma, 1983
Chalk Hill, 1989
Dry Creek Valley, 1983
Fort Ross - Seaview, 2011
Fountaingrove District, 2011
Green Valley of Russian River Valley, 1983
Knights Valley, 1983
Moon Mountain, 2013
Northern Sonoma, 1990
Petaluma Gap, 2018
Pine Mountain - Cloverdale Peak, 2011
Rockpile, 2002
Russian River Valley, 1983
Sonoma Coast, 1987
Sonoma Mountain, 1985
Sonoma Valley, 1981
West Sonoma Coast. 2022

Chapter 2: Getting Around Sonoma

From the Golden Gate Bridge, southern Sonoma County is a thirty-minute drive north through Marin County. As compared to urban San Francisco and suburban Marin, Sonoma is made up of small towns, farms, ranches and vineyards, fit between oaks, laurels, pines and expansive redwood forests.

Sonoma produces vegetables for their many restaurants, apples in the Russian River Valley, small grows of cannabis, hops for their renowned craft beers, dairy for their artisan cheeses, Petaluma's prized poultry, and beef cattle grazing the bucolic, green hills of coastal Sonoma, plus honey from their many flowers.

But premium wine grapes are their biggest crop, grown in nineteen American Viticulture Areas (AVAs), spread across a county more than twice as big as Napa. Not surprisingly, winemaking is their biggest industry with over five hundred wineries. The most visited wine regions are Los Carneros, Sonoma Valley, Russian River Valley, Dry Creek Valley and Alexander Valley.

The differences between the various growing regions are remarkable, thanks to Sonoma's two coastlines: one along the cold, deep Pacific Ocean, and another along the shallow San Pablo Bay. Their influence makes every valley, line of hills and mountain slope climatically unique.

These sit atop a checkerboard of diverse geological structures, caused by the meeting of volcanic uprisings and ancient basalt seabeds cut by numerous rivers and streams. The result is the world's most varied premium wine region, that grows over a hundred grape varietals.

In comparison, Burgundy France produces primarily four or five varietals, Champagne produces three, Bordeaux about ten and Napa about fifteen. Sonoma's coastal Pinot Noir and Chardonnay compete well with Burgundy. The Cabernet Sauvignon and Merlot of Alexander Valley hold their own against Napa and Bordeaux.

Even less widely planted grapes like Sangiovese, Grenache and Zinfandel, produce wines that compare well to the places where those grapes have grown for centuries. Sonoma was able to accomplish this since the 1820's, when the first vines were planted, due to its remarkable location.

This same combination of terrains, crossed by hills and waterways, makes navigating the region challenging. But when you know what to expect, it becomes easier.

What's in a Name?

Let's start with the name Sonoma, which signifies the 'Valley of the Moon', and it applies to the crescent-shaped, fifteen-mile long Sonoma Valley, that is bisected by Highway 12, Sonoma Highway, and bordered by Arnold Drive to the west, which you can often take to avoid traffic congestion.

Sonoma is also the name of the little city that sits at the base of the valley, so often, when people say they are going to Sonoma, that's where they mean. It is also the name of the county, which is bordered by Marin to the south, Mendocino to the north, Napa to the east, and the cold, Pacific Ocean to the west, which sends fog banks sweeping over the land nightly. So, when you say you are going to 'Sonoma', it helps to be specific!

For wine touring, we divide the county into North and South. The historic town of Sonoma is the center of the southern half and elegant Healdsburg is the center of the northern half. The city of Santa Rosa, which spreads over a wide plain, is the economic midpoint. When deciding on a day trip, for the sake of time and distance, plan to visit wineries in either one region or the other.

The Important Roads You Need to Know

Highway 101

Highway 101 is a major highway that crosses the Golden Gate Bridge from San Francisco and intersects **Highway 37** abeam of southern Sonoma. **Hwy 101** also intersects **Highway 12** in Santa Rosa and further north, River Road, which travels west through the Russian River Valley. **Hwy 101** also intersects **Healdsburg Avenue** and **Dry Creek Road** which connects to the northern most wine valleys, Dry Creek and Alexander.

Highway 37 starts at **Highway 101** and travels east, ending in Solano County at **Highway 80**. It intersects **Highway 121** North at Sears Point (Landmark: Sonoma Raceway and the 'turbo cow'). **Highway 121** is home to numerous popular Los Carneros wineries, and it intersects **Highway 12 North**, which goes north to downtown Sonoma and the Valley. *Taking **Highway 101N** to **37E** to **121N** to **12N** is the quickest and prettiest way from the Golden Gate Bridge to downtown Sonoma.*

Highway 121 is combined with **Highway 12** for a short distance, before continuing east into Napa County and intersecting **Highway 29**, Napa's main road.

Highway 12 travels North through downtown Sonoma. It continues north into the heart of the 'Valley of the Moon', including the towns of Glen Ellen and Kenwood. It goes through the outskirts of the city of Santa Rosa where it intersects **Highway 101**. Then it continues west into downtown Sebastopol, intersecting **Highway 116**.

Highway 116 also intersects **Highway 121** in Los Carneros and merges with **Highway 101** in Petaluma. It then splits off in Cotati and goes northwest through Sebastopol. Then it travels through the Russian River Valley as **Gravenstein Highway**.

It passes through Guerneville and becomes River Road, heading west until it ends at **Highway 1, the Pacific Coast Highway**.

River Road intersects **Highway 101** north of Santa Rosa. It travels on the river's southern bank, through the heart of the Russian River Valley, ending at the **Pacific Coast Highway**.

Healdsburg Avenue intersects **Highway 101**. The 'Downtown' exit brings you to Westside Road, which travels south into the northern part of the Russian River Valley. Going north on **Healdsburg Avenue** brings you through the downtown. Then it intersects **Dry Creek Road** which goes north into the Dry Creek Valley.

Healdsburg Avenue also continues north through the west side of the Alexander valley. North of town it intersects **Alexander Valley Road**, which goes into the eastern side of the valley and continues south into northern Napa.

A Helpful Note About Very Convenient Los Carneros

The thin slice of land at the top of the San Pablo Bay, that spans Sonoma and Napa is called Los Carneros. Its wind-whipped, basaltic, highly drained vineyards are planted like a carpet with Pinot Noir and Chardonnay, in a continuous swath of precise green lines.

The area got its name from an early 1800's Spanish land grant, because the cool winds blowing off the bay make these rolling hills a good place to raise 'los carneros', or sheep. It is unique among the North Bay American Viticulture Areas (AVA) because it is shared by two counties, Napa and Sonoma, but the consistent climate, geology and exposure make the designation appropriate on both sides of the county line.

Los Carneros has often been called the American Burgundy because it produces so much of America's premium Pinot Noir and Chardonnay, although the strong winds produce a higher acid wine that goes best with food. Truthfully, Sonoma's Russian River and Pacific Coast wines may represent a truer comparison to Burgundy's earthy style.

But Los Carneros is home to some wonderful wineries and well worth the visit for their bright and refreshing wines. The fact that it is so convenient to San Francisco makes it a popular daytrip destination. Many of the first 'Carneros' wineries you encounter in Sonoma coming north see hordes of visitors, so they price their wines accordingly. But when you go a little ways off the beaten path you will find numerous premium producers.

Navigating Sonoma is easy because there are not many roads, but the actual driving can be tricky because wine country roads tend to be narrow, winding and sometimes bordered by thick forests. So, take your time, enjoy the scenery and be safe!

Popular Routes

Chapter 3: Quick ABC's for Tasting Wine

The way you drink wine with a meal is different from how you sample it in a tasting room. The funny techniques you see people using during tastings help them perceive the wine better through the senses of sight, scent and taste. It starts with the glassware. Wineries use crystal goblets because they are rougher than glass. When you swirl the wine, those microscopic bumps pull apart its molecules, mixing them with oxygen, releasing the aromas and flavors for you to experience. Hold the glass by the stem because that makes it easier to move the wine around inside the glass. Fancier wineries have fancier glasses.

Start by holding the glass upright and taking a sniff. Much of what you're smelling is alcohol rising off the liquid. Next, set the glass on the tabletop, place your fingers firmly on top of the base and vigorously swirl the wine. Now, pick the glass up and hold it at a 45-degree angle and put your nose on the glass' lower lip, and take a sniff.

Because the alcohol fumes are rising in the globe and slipping out the upper edge, bypassing your nose, you're smelling the pure fruit flavors below, the wonderful scent of fermented grapes! Sip the wine and move it around your mouth, so it touches all your taste buds from the tip of your tongue to the valley in its center, and then, both sides.

Once the flavors are well dispersed, swallow the sip. Repeat this process until there is none left. Note that there are scent notes that are only released when they touch your tongue. To access them, gently breathe in through your mouth so the aromas on your palate reach your nose via the back of your throat. There is another quality you should note called 'mouth feel'. It is how the texture of the wine feels to the surface of your mouth. Is it sharply acidic, soothingly silky, or almost sticky and syrupy? One 'mouth feel' to watch out for is the almost flame-like touch of a high alcohol, dry wine, which is why that kind of wine is called 'hot'.

Port is also high in alcohol, but the wine is heavy and sweet, so the alcohol is deeply embedded in the flavors. But, many Zinfandels and Cabernets are very hot, at 15% to 16% alcohol, while dry (meaning that all the grape sugar has been converted to alcohol). If the dehydrating alcohol is not well moderated and integrated into the wine, it will feel like a sip dries out your tongue and you may be thirstier after the tasting than before you began. With those wines the alcohol may have been concentrated on the surface by the swirling. You may be able to fix that by holding the glass almost horizontally and gently rolling it for twenty or thirty seconds. This may help re-integrate the alcohol into the liquid and soften the mouth feel.

Wine Geek Alert! There is an odd phenomenon that happens with wines that have been aged in oak for an extended period, usually eighteen months or more. As related to me by winemakers, when you swirl the wine clockwise you will smell predominantly fruit flavors. But when you swirl counterclockwise, you will also notice the nutty, sometimes spicy flavors that come from the barrel. Why does this happen? According to Ralph's best quasi-scientific analysis, it is due to the relative efficiency of vortices. A clockwise swirl more efficiently mixes the various part of the wine together. But the less efficient counterclockwise swirl allows the layers to separate. The wooden barrel flavors are the last ones to be infused into the juice and in this less organized mix, some of those woody notes are left floating at the top for your nose to discover. This technique is used by some winemakers to determine a barrel's influence on the wine. If you have a good sense of smell, you will notice the difference. Now you are officially a Wine Geek!

Chapter 4: Winery Directory

A. Rafanelli Winery – A Popular Dry Creek Winery – Wines: Cabernet Sauvignon, Merlot, Zinfandel – 4685 W. Dry Creek Rd. Healdsburg CA 95448 – Dry Creek Valley – www.arafanelliwinery.com – (707) 433-1385 – (parties over 6) cash/check only – Hours: 10:00am to 4:00pm – Appointment – No Tours – This is a popular winery, and they enjoy tremendous loyalty from their customers. The casual tasting is done in the barrel room or outside in the garden and often by a family member. There is a gate at the bottom of the driveway. Navigation: They are located on the left side of the road just north of Lambert Bridge Road. Map J

Abbot's Passage & Mercantile – Sonoma Valley – Wines: Rhone Varietals and Blends – 777 Madrone Road, Glen Ellen, CA 95442 – www.abbotspassage.com – (707) 939-3017 – Hours: 11:00pm to 5:00pm Thursdays – Monday – info@abbotspassage.com. This big, rambling winery five miles north of the Plaza is one of the more historic parts of California's Wine Country. The land surrounding the winery has been planted to vineyards since 1860. There is a 400-year-old Bay tree out behind the winery. They have a spacious, comfortable culinary tasting, with a lovely gift section focused on products from women owned businesses. The wines are well made. They are just one minute off of Route 12 on Madrone Road, which is a traffic light with Hamel Winery on the right. Map D

Acaibo Trinite Estate (Lurton Family) – Alexander Valley - Chalk Hill – a Cross of Bordeaux and California – 10603 Chalk Hill Rd, Healdsburg, CA 95448 – website – (707) 791-0943 – Hours: Tours and Tastings by Appointment – High end producer, – Map G

Acorn Winery – South Eastern Russian River – Field Blends – Wines: Sangiovese, Dolcetto, Cabernet Franc, Zinfandel, Syrah, Blends – 12040 Old Redwood Highway. Healdsburg CA 95448 www.acornwinery.com – (707) 433-6440 – Hours: Appointment – The property was first planted to grapes in the 1850's. They produce some field blends, a traditional method where the numerous varietals are planted together and then combined in the tanks. They are located down a long, narrow drive, leading to an odd collection of buildings, and a partially open–air tasting room. They have a loyal following and well–made wines. Their sign is located north of the drive for Rodney Strong and the J Winery on the opposite (east) side of the road. The sign is not large, so take your time as you get close. Map G

Adobe Road Winery – Tasting Room on the Petaluma River Front – Wines: Cabernet Franc, Cabernet Sauvignon, Meritage, Petite Syrah, Pinot Noir, Sauvignon Blanc, Syrah, Zinfandel, Port – 6 Petaluma Blvd North Suite A1 in the Great Petaluma Mill, Petaluma, CA – www.adoberoadwines.com – (707) 774-6699 – Hours: 11:00am to 7:00pm – This long time Petaluma winery opened a tasting room in their downtown for their wonderful wines. It is owned by the sports car racer, Kevin Buckler. The winery is in the nearby corporate park, along with some of his race cars.

Aesthete Winery & Farm – Dry Creek Valley Charming – Wines: Zinfandel, Petite Syrah, Dessert – 5610 Dry Creek Rd. Healdsburg CA 95448 – www.truethurst st.com – (707) 433-9545 – Hours: 11:00am–5:00pm – This winery grows their grapes in a Biodynamic way, and their property includes diverse gardens, fruit trees, a beautiful patio, and a seating area along side the Dry Creek, which is not always dry. In fact, they often see trout swimming there. The tasting room is spacious and well lit, with two tasting bars. The staff is great, knowledgeable, engaged and fun. This is a partnership of three expert wine industry professionals and they've done a great job putting it together. This is also where the VML wines are being poured as of 2021. Map J

Alexander Valley Vineyards – Charming Old Style Sonoma – Wines: Gewürztraminer, Chardonnay, Viognier, Pinot Noir, Sangiovese, Zinfandel, Merlot, Cabernet Sauvignon – 8644 Highway 128 Healdsburg CA 95448 – www.avvwine.com – (707) 433-7209 – Hours: 10:00am – 5:00pm – Cave Tours – Wine and Cheese Pairings This is a friendly winery with a great staff, a cute gift shop and some good wines and they do reserve tastings and a vineyard hike by appointment. It has that wonderfully inclusive feeling that we love about Northern Sonoma. They have caves, which makes sense, since they are tucked up against a hillside in the southern part of the Alexander Valley, close to the Hanna winery. They have a nice variety of wines that are moderately priced. Map N

Amista Vineyards – Dry Creek Charm – Wines: Chardonnay, Rose of Syrah, Syrah, Zinfandel, Cabernet Sauvignon – 3320 Dry Creek Road Healdsburg CA 95448 – www.amistavineyards.com – (707) 431-9200 – Hours: 11:00am – 4:30pm – Their 'barn' is surrounded by 20 acres of their own Chardonnay and Syrah vines on the gravel rich floor of the Dry Creek Valley. Their Zinfandel and Cabernet Sauvignon grapes come from local growers. The tasting room is spacious with great views of the vineyards outside and a relaxed, friendly style. Map J

Amapola Creek Vineyards and Winery – Sonoma Valley Hillside – Wines: Cabernet Sauvignon – Tasting Room next to VJB at 9077 Sonoma Highway, Kenwood, CA 95452 Estate: 392 London Way, Sonoma, CA 95476 – www.amapolacreek.com – (707) 938-3783 – Hours: 10:00am to 3:00pm Thursday – Monday – The home winery of Richard Arrowood, an iconic winemaker working exclusively in Sonoma County for more than for 50+ years. From 1974 through 1990, he created the wines for Chateau St. Jean, where he developed some of the first vineyard–designate Chardonnay and Cabernet Sauvignon produced in Sonoma County. Owned by B. Wise. Map D

Amphora Winery – Dry Creek Valley at the Timber Creek Center – Wines: Petite Syrah, Zinfandel, Pinot Noir, Merlot, Cabernet Sauvignon, Syrah, Chardonnay – 4791 Dry Creek Rd. Bldg. 6 Healdsburg CA 95448 – www.amphorawines.com – (707) 431-7767 – Hours: 11:00am to 4:30pm – Groups by Appointment – This is a wonderful little winery located in a big white building just a short walk from Papapietro–Perry, Peterson and Kokomo. The winemaker was previously a potter and the tasting room also serves as a gallery. During harvest, women visitors can sometimes crush grapes with their feet, Lucy style. Those 'Lucy' wine proceeds benefit a charity.

This is a fun winery to visit, a good value and the winemaker/owner is often around, if not pouring. Map L

Anaba Wines – Los Carneros on the Main Road – Wines: Chardonnay, Pinot Noir, Viognier, Rhone style blends – 60 Bonneau St. Sonoma CA 95476 – (707) 996-4188 – Hours: 11:00am–5:00pm – As you come up from San Francisco over the Golden Gate Bridge, Anaba is among the first dozen wineries you encounter in Los Carneros. They are at the intersection with the flashing light north of the Racetrack and just past the gas station. Turn left there and then right into their parking lot. Their winery and vineyards are behind the tasting room which is cute, comfortable, welcoming and surprisingly quiet despite being at a busy intersection. They make good wines. Map A

Annadel Estate Winery – Sonoma Valley Boutique – Wines: Bordeaux and Burgundy Blends, General French – 6687 Sonoma Highway, Santa Rosa, CA 95409 – www.annadelestatewinery.com – (707) 537-8007 – Hours: 11:00am–5:00pm – Appointment – This pretty, bucolic winery is owned and operated by two sommeliers. It sits on a property dating back to the 1880's. They also have five acres devoted to flowers and they host small weddings and events. Map D

Arista Winery – Estate Recently Sold - Russian River at the Edge of Dry Creek – Wines: Pinot Noir, Chardonnay – 7015 Westside Rd. Healdsburg CA 95448 – www.aristawinery.com – (707) 473-0606 – Hours: 11:00am–5:00pm Appointment – This is a small, pretty winery tucked in the western hillsides south of the town of Healdsburg. They have an intimate tasting room, surrounded by comfortable tables that are nested in the gardens, built around huge boulders, with a distinctly Zen feeling. There is a great place to picnic under the trees by prearrangement. The tasting is pleasant, and the staff is relaxed and friendly. The wines, over the years have moved into the upper premium region. Map H Check Website for update.

Armida Winery – At the Edge of Russian River and Dry Creek Valleys with Great Views – Wines: Rosé, Pinot Noir, Chardonnay, Zinfandel, Gewürztraminer, Sauvignon Blanc, Cabernet Sauvignon – 2201 Westside Rd. Healdsburg CA 95448 – www.armidawinery.com – (707) 433-2222 – Hours: 11:00am–5:00pm – The Geodesic Dome winery sits on top of a hill with great views of the Russian River Valley. The tasting room is bright and spacious with some interesting gifts and the staff is friendly. There are gardens, patios and picnic areas. The wine list includes a nice variety, reasonably priced in a part of the valley that has become increasingly expensive. Map H

Arrowood Vineyards – Sonoma Valley – Shares a driveway with the Imagery Winery – Wines: Chardonnay, Pinot Blanc, Viognier, Gewürztraminer, Merlot, Cabernet Sauvignon, Syrah, Riesling – 14347 Sonoma Highway. Glen Ellen CA 95442 – www.arrowoodwinery.com – (707) 935-2600 – Hours: 10:00am to 4:30pm – This is a pretty property and a charming tasting room just six miles north of the Sonoma Plaza. They have nice outdoor patios and a good gift shop, although the tastings have always been done inside. The winery is surrounded by its vineyards. The staff is knowledgeable and friendly. They are owned by the Jackson Family. Map D

Auteur – Sonoma Plaza – Wines: Bordeaux and Burgundy – 373 1st St. West, Sonoma, CA 95476 – www.auteurwines.com – (707)–938-9211 Hours: 10:00am to 5:30pm Appointment – This is a premium tasting room by appointment just steps off the Sonoma Plaza. This is part of a growing community of high-end producers of small lot wines that are choosing to locate in the convenient downtown, rather than deal with the complications of setting up their tasting room at a winery or vineyard. They are located just around the corner from the Girl and the Fig Restaurant on Map C

B Wise Vineyards – Sonoma Valley with Two Locations – Wines: Bordeaux and Burgundy Blends – 9077 Sonoma Highway. Kenwood CA 95452 – www.bwisevineyards.com – 707-282-9169 – Hours: 10:30am to 4:30pm – lounge@bwisevineyards.com – This is a high-end winery in the mid-Sonoma Valley with two locations, a tasting room on Highway 29 and a small cave built into the eastern hillsides near their home and offices. They also own a winery in Napa. Their tasting room is shown on Map D

B.R. Cohn Winery – Sonoma Valley with Grapevines, Olives and Music – Wines: Cabernet Sauvignon, Zinfandel, Chardonnay, Merlot, Syrah – 15000 Sonoma Highway Glen Ellen CA 95442 – www.brcohn.com (707) 938-4064 – Hours: 10:00am to 5:00pm – Tours by Appointment – This is five miles north of the Plaza on a picture-perfect hillside, surrounded by vines and olive groves. The building was once a stagecoach stop for the Sonoma to Santa Rosa run, that was transformed into a home by Bruce Cohn, a native of this area, and the manager of the Doobie Brothers. Later, as the winery expanded, it became the tasting room for the winery outback. They have both inside and outside tasting areas, a separate gift shop for their olive oils and related products, and picnic tables. Behind the winery is a large event space, that is coupled with a spot in the vineyards to accommodate weddings. During the summer they also host concerts, that have continued even though the Cohn family no longer owns the property. Map D

Bacchus – South Healdsburg – Wines: A varety from several wineries – 14210 Bacchus Landing Way, Healdsburg, CA 95448 – www.bacchuslanding.com – (707) 799-1821 – Hours: 10:00am to 5:00pm – Opened in 2021 this is a large space that hosts about five winery tasting rooms with inside and outside spaces off Westside Road by downtown Healdsburg. Map H

Bacigalupi Vineyards – Russian River Valley on Westside Road – Wines: Burgundy Blends, General French – 4353 Westside Road Healdsburg, CA 95448 – www.bacigalupivineyards.com – (707) 473-0115 – Hours: 11:00am to 4:30pm – tastingroom@bacigalupivineyards.com – This is a small, friendly hospitality building tucked just off Westside Road, in a hollow below their revered vineyards. Why are they revered? Because they were one of the main sources for the chardonnay grapes that went into the Chateau Montelena Chardonnay that won at the 1976 Judgment of Paris. There is a great photo showing Grandma Bacigalupi standing with the winemaker Mike Grgich, next to the tall vines. When we first started visiting this tasting room, hosted by the family, the original vines were still there, although the vineyard had since been replanted. One of the great ironies in wine country is that while it was two Napa wineries that won at that famous wine tasting, the grapes for the Chardonnay were mostly from their sister county Sonoma. Map H

Balletto Vineyards – Southern Russian River Valley Outside Sebastopol – Cozy Tasting Room – Wines: Chardonnay, Pinot Grigio, Pinot Gris, Pinot Noir, Rosé of Pinot Noir, Syrah. Gewürztraminer, Zinfandel – 5700 Occidental Rd. Santa Rosa CA 95401 – www.ballettovineyards.com – (707) 568-2455 – Hours: 10:00am–5:00pm Appointment – Balleto has numerous vineyards in this part of the southern Russian River Valley. They are located down a long gravel road in a pretty, flat part of the valley between Santa Rosa and Sebastopol. The winery is a steel warehouse building surrounded by vines, but they have a pretty outdoor sitting area, and the tasting room is cute and cozy, with some nice gifts and a friendly staff. The experience is relaxed, and the wines are good and true to the area. Map I

Banshee Winery – Mid-Alexander Valley – Wines: Pinot Noir and Chardonnay from Sonoma Coast and Anderson Valley in Mendocino – 5110 Highway 128 Geyserville CA 95448 – www.bansheewines.com – (707) 395-0915 – Hours: 10:00–5:00pm closed Tues & Wed– They are located in a very modern building with great views and wonderful picnic areas. This award-winning building would be enough of a reason to come here. From their tasting room you can look through the panoramic windows, stroll out onto the patios, or peer down into their cavernous barrel cellar where they often host events at banquet tables. They are nearby the Robert Young Winery, the Hawkes Winery, and Stonestreet. Map O

Bartholomew Park Winery – Southern Sonoma Valley east of the Plaza with a Park – Wines: Sauvignon Blanc, Merlot, Syrah, Zinfandel, Cabernet Sauvignon – 1000 Vineyard Lane Sonoma CA 95476 – www.bartpark.com – (707) 935-9511 – Hours: 11:00am to 4:30pm – They are located just to the east of downtown Sonoma and it includes a lovely picnic grounds. Around 2020 the winery changed owners and the entire experience went through a dramatic upgrade and now tastings are offered inside and out on a lovely oak knoll. Allow time to visit the gallery, it is a wonderful space to enjoy art. This building has a long history, including being the local hospital, and a home for wayward women sent from San Francisco, which of course caused all kinds of chaos for the locals. The original property, owned by the Bartholomew family was deeded for the public good many years ago as a park, and the winery and vineyards are residents. The next property over is Buena Vista, one of California's most historic wineries, so you can combine the two into a very convenient day. Map A

Battaglini Estate Winery – Southern Russian River Near Olivet Road – Wines: Zinfandel, Chardonnay, Petite Sirah – 2948 Piner Road, Santa Rosa, CA 95401 – www.battaglini-wines.com (707) 318-8944 – Hours: 10:00am to 5:00pm Appointment – This is very much a small family winery, producing about 2500 cases of good wine, on land that has been farmed to grapes since the late 1800's. There is an Italian style to the place and a homey feel. This area has been known for growing great Zinfandel since grape growing began here. They are nearby DeLoach, Inman Family and Harvest Moon. Map I

Bella Wine Caves – Northwestern Dry Creek Valley – Wines: Zinfandel, Syrah – 9711 W. Dry Creek Road. CA 95448 – www.BellaWinery.com – (707) 473-9171 – Hours: 11:00am to 4:30pm – This is a small, charming family–run winery located up a narrow road at the top of the Dry Creek Valley. The tasting is in their caves that are dug into the hillsides beneath their vineyards. Whenever there is a special weekend, such as the Barrel Tasting or Passport, this is always a favorite stop for those in the know. It is pet friendly and has accessible picnic tables on the lawn with wonderful views of the valley. The caves are especially nice on a hot day. Map L

Beltane Ranch – Sonoma Valley with an Historic B&B – Wines: Sauvignon Blanc and Zinfandel – 11775 Sonoma Highway, Glen Ellen, CA 95442 – www.beltaneranch.com – (707) 833-4233 – Hours: Appointment – This is a B&B at a House built in 1892 on a 105 Acres that sells wines from their vineyards. The site was the home of Mary Ellen Johnson. an important Abolitionist and one San Francisco's wealthiest women. Map D

Bennett Valley Cellars – Sonoma Plaza tasting room – Wines: Bordeaux and Burgundy Blends – 127 E Napa St, Sonoma, CA 95476 – www.bennettvalleycellars.com – (707) 934-8173 – Hours: 12:00pm – 6:00pm. They are next door to the Maya restaurant shown on Map C.

Benovia Winery – Southern Russian River – Wines: Pinot Noir, Chardonnay – 3339 Hartman Road Santa Rosa, CA 95401 – www.benoviawinery.com – (707) 921-1040 – Hours: 10:00am to 3:30pm Appointment – This is a charming, family run winery surrounded by their vines just east of Olivet Lane, nearby DeLoach and Inman Family. They see limited numbers of guests by appointment. Map I

Benziger Family Winery – Sonoma Valley Biodynamic Advocates & Tram Tours – Wines: Sauvignon Blanc, Chardonnay, Pinot Noir, Cabernet Sauvignon, Merlot, Syrah, Muscat, Port. 1883 London Ranch Rd. Glen Ellen CA 95442 – www.benziger.com – (707) 935-4527 – This is a great winery experience, Biodynamic/Organic, Caves, Gardens, Gifts, picnic tables, and the best tours in Sonoma. A tractor pulls passenger laden trams up into the Biodynamic Vineyards for a great lecture, followed by tours of the caves and the winery. Tours run on the 1/2 hour, starting at 11, except 12:30, until 3. They have added a Partner's Tour that goes more deeply into the vineyards and their approach to agriculture. Map D

Blue Rock – Alexander Valley – Merlot, Cabernet Sauvignon – 24509 Rich Ranch Rd, Cloverdale, CA 95425 – bluerockvineyard.com – (707) 486-9661 – Hours: 10-3:30 Appointment – Very Small and exclusive family winery with gourmet lunch, beautiful location – Map M

Bonneau Wines – Los Carneros on the Main Road at the Carneros Deli – Wines: Cabernet Sauvignon, Zinfandel, Chardonnay, Malbec, Petite Syrah, Meritage – 23001 Arnold Drive, Sonoma CA 95476 www.bonneauwine.com – (800) 996-0420 – Hours: 11:00am–6:00pm – The Bonneau family came from Bordeaux in the 1920's and has farmed this land since then. Since the 1990s, they have been selling grapes to other wineries. In 2002, they introduced their own wines and they also source grapes from some of the area's best vineyards. It helps to know the right people. It is a low-key location attached to their deli so get a snack at the same time. Map A

Bricoleur Vineyards - Southern Russian River – A wide selection from Northern Sonoma including Pinot Noir, Zinfandel, Petite Sirah, Cabernet Sauvignon and Sparking Wines – 7394 Starr Rd, Windsor, CA 95492 - bricoleurvineyards.com – (707) 857-5700 - Appointment - Beautiful location on the flats to the south of the river, by folks with historic connections to the local wine industry. Map I.

Buena Vista Winery – Sonoma Valley East of the Plaza with History – Wines: Pinot Gris, Chardonnay, Pinot Noir, Merlot, Syrah, Port – 18000 Old Winery Rd. Sonoma CA 95476 – www.BuenaVistaCarneros.com – (800) 926–1266 – (707) 265-1472 – Hours: 10:00am to 5:00pm – This is California's most historic winery, founded in 1857 just minutes from the old town of Sonoma. The fragrant Eucalyptus trees that line the winding road lead you there. It is an extraordinary property and the original buildings have been beautifully restored. There are historic tours, special tastings and fun education. The winery has wooden tanks on the main floor and a tool library on the top floor. The restoration of the main winery was an amazing project and the place is unique. Map A

Campana Ranch Wines – Southern Russian River – Pinot Noir, Cabernet Franc, Cabernet Sauvignon – Blends - - region - 3631 Mark West Station Rd, Windsor, CA 95492 - www.campanaranchwines.com - (707) 337-0844 – Appointment – This is a very small winery producing less than a thousand cases year. The couple who own it have many years of experience managing vineyards for large companies, and everything they make is hand done. It is a lovely country experience, with horse and dogs and vines. Map I

Calluna Vineyards – Chalk Hill – Sauv Blanc, Merlot, Malbec, Cab Sauv – 11450 Brooks Rd, Windsor, CA 95492 – callunavineyards.com – (707) 239-1325 – hours: 10-4 – This is a premium Cabernet style producer in a beautiful, if remote part of Chalk Hill – Map G

Capo Creek – Dry Creek Valley – Zinfandel – 7171 W Dry Creek Rd, Healdsburg, CA 95448 – website – (707) 608-8448 – Hours: 10-5 Appointment - Small family winery, lovely grounds, the owner often hosts– Map J

Carpenter Vineyards – Alexander Valley- Chalk Hill – Pinot Noir, Chardonnay, Semillion – 14255 Chalk Hill Rd, Healdsburg, CA 95448 – carpenterwine.com – (707) 385-8177 – Hours: 11-6 Appointment - Small winery, beautiful location, great wines and a food pairing – Map M

Cast Winery – Northern Dry Creek Valley – Bordeaux, Burgundy Blends, Zinfandel, Petite Sirah – 8500 Dry Creek Road Geyserville CA 95441 – Wines: – www.castwines.com – (707) 431-1225 – Hours: 10:00am to 5:00pm – Appointment – A small family-owned winery in an especially pretty part of the valley just south of Ferrari Carano. Map L

Chalk Hill Estate Winery – North Eastern Russian River South of Alexander Valley in the Chalk Hill District – Beautiful Setting – Wines: Chardonnay, Sauvignon Blanc, Pinot Gris, Cabernet Sauvignon, Merlot, Semillon, Blends – 10300 Chalk Hill Rd. Healdsburg CA 95448 – www.chalkhill.com – (707) 838-4306 – Hours: 10:00am–4:00pm This is a stately winery in a gorgeous location that makes wonderful wines. The building is grand and the tasting is excellent. The Chalk Hill section is known for its white, rocky soil, which you can see jutting out of the cuts along the roads. This is a great place to bring your camera. Map G

Char Vale Vineyards – Southern Russian River – Pinot Noir, Chardonnay – 9280 Occidental Rd, Sebastopol, CA 95472 – website – (707) 827-6102 – Hours:11-4:30 – Most of the wines are from the Green Valley part of the Russian River Valley. This is a hidden gem just south of Graton. These are small batch wines poured by a friendly team. – Map G

Chateau Diana – Northern Dry Creek Valley – Wines: A wide and fun variety – 6195 Dry Creek Road Healdsburg, CA 95448 – www.chateaud.com – 707-433-6993 Hours: 11-5 Closed Tuesdays – This is a relaxed tasting room in a lovely location that believes in hospitality. Map J

Chateau Saint Jean Winery – Queen of the Sonoma Valley – Wines: Pinot Blanc, Chardonnay, Viognier, Pinot Noir, Merlot, Malbec, Cabernet Sauvignon – 8555 Sonoma Highway, Kenwood CA 95452 – www.chateaustjean.com – (707) 833-4134 Hours: 10:00am–5:00pm – This is a Sonoma Valley favorite because of the great architecture, gardens, gift shop, deli/market and tours. They have two tasting rooms, the regular and the reserve in the wood lined mansion. The staff is friendly and knowledgeable. It is a popular, well distributed label that you'll find easily when you get home. The property was owned originally by a couple from Michigan, and they created a pond next to the mansion in the shape of the Great Lakes with Michigan in the center. Over time, the pond broke down and now that's been replaced with a patio, filled with comfortable table seating. The main tasting room is where you will also find the deli and restrooms. The Mansion Reserve Tasting room also has outdoor seating by request. It is a elegant experience. Map D

Christopher Creek Winery – Southern Russian River Valley – Family Grape Growers – 641 Limerick Lane Healdsburg CA 95448 – www.christophercreek.com – (707) 433-2001 – Hours: 11:00am–5:00pm Appointment – The Wasserman family has been growing grapes and other types of fruit in this section of the Russian River Valley for many years and they give much of the credit for their excellent wines to the quality of their grapes. It is a charming winery, a small tasting room, relaxed and friendly with lovely views of the hills. Map G

Claypool Cellars – Southern Russian River – Reisling, Pinot Noir, Sparkling – 5425 Gravenstein Hwy N, Sebastopol, CA 95472 – www.purplepachyderm.com – (707) 820-1263 Hours: 11:30-5:30 Closed Tuesdays – Their fun and relaxed tasting room, filled with antiques, just south of Forestville, with a patio out back and a hot dog maker, if you catch it on the right days. – Map G

Cline Cellars – Los Carneros just off the Main Road – History and Diversity – Wines: Mourvèdre, Carignane, Syrah, Zinfandel, Viognier, Marsanne, Roussanne, Blends – 24737 Arnold Dr. Sonoma CA 95476 – www.clinecellars.com –

(707) 940-4000 – Hours: 10:00am–6:00pm – Tours – This was the original site of the San Francisco Solano mission, the 21st and final Mission established in California. Later the mission was moved to the Sonoma Plaza. It is a great location, and the grounds are expansive and park–like. They do tours and have a bird and animal collection. They built a charming museum for antique scale models of the 21 Franciscan Missions. The tasting room is homey and friendly, and popular, especially late in the day, because they are on the right side of the road as people are leaving the valleys to return to the city. The wines are always good, and they make a wide variety. Fred Cline was one of the first people in the area to use sheep for grazing as part of their vineyard management which is not only 'Green' but cute. The winery is run on solar and there is an educational display about that. The buildings make you feel like you're at a country farm. Map A

Clos Du Bois Wines – CLOSED AS OF 2021 – Alexander Valley – 19410 Geyserville Ave. Geyserville CA 95441 –

Colagrossi Wines – Downtown Windsor – Wines: Specializing in Italian Varietals – 7755 Bell Road Windsor CA – www.colagrossiwines.com – (707) 529-5459 – Hours: Appointment – They produce 1000 cases of wines yearly, made by the owner. Not shown on map.

Collier Falls Vineyard – Dry Creek Valley – Wines: Bordeaux and Burgundy Blends, Zinfandel, Petite Sirah – 4791 Dry Creek Road, Bldg 11 Healdsburg , CA 95448 – www.collier-falls.com – (707) 433-0100 Hours: Appointment – This is a wonderful couple who started it in the late 1990's and produces wines from their own twenty acres. Check with them about where they are currently offering tastings.

Comstock Wines – Dry Creek Valley – Wines: Bordeaux, Burgundy, Zinfandel, Grenache, General French – 1290 Dry Creek Road Healdsburg, CA 95448 – www.comstockwines.com – (707) 723-3011 – Hours: 10:30am to 4:30pm – A spacious winery with a lovely terrace overlooking their Merlot vineyards on the valley floor, convenient to downtown Healdsburg. Map J

Copain – Russian River Valley on Eastside Road south of Healdsburg – Wines: Pinot Noir, Chardonnay, Syrah, Picpoul, Trousseau – 7800 Eastside Road Healdsburg, CA 95448 – www.copainwines.com – (707) 837-8822 – Hours: 12:00am to 3:00pm – Appointment – A small ultra-premium producer on the east side of the Russian River in an area with very few wineries. A lovely location and a gracious experience. Map H

Coturri Winery – Western Sonoma Valley – Wines: Very interesting Blends, General French – 6725 Enterprise Road Glen Ellen, CA 95442 – www.coturriwinery.com – Hours: Appointment – tony@coturriwinery.com – the Coturri family are well-known as organic growers who manage numerous other properties besides their own. Their own wines are unique blends which includes an apple cider. They are tucked away in the rolling hills to the west of the Sonoma Valley and Glen Ellen and south of Bennett Valley Road. Map D

Croix Estate Winery – Southern Russian River – Pinot Noir, Chardonnay – 1406 Wood Rd, Fulton, CA 95439 –www.croix-estate.com – (707) 595-3803 – Hours: 10-4 Appointment – Beautiful grounds, private tastings. This is owned by Kirk Venge, one of Napa's favorite consulting winemakers. The first vintage was 2012. These are small batches of premium wines. They are open to tastings for collectors – Map G

D'Argenzio – Santa Rosa Office Park Location – Wines: A very wide variety with a focus on Italian varietals – 1301 Cleveland Ave Suite D, Santa Rosa, CA 95401 – www.dargenziowine.com – (707) 546-2466 Hours: Monday – Tuesday Appointment, Wednesday, Thursday, and Sunday 11:00am–5:00pm, Friday–Saturday 11:00am to 7:00pm – reservations@dargenziowine.com – D'Argenzio Winery is owned and operated by Ray and Ricci D'Argenzio (twin brothers) with Ray's daughter, Breanna Tamburin, running the Santa Rosa wine tasting room. They offer wine tastings, tours, antipasti boards, wood–fired pizza, bocce ball, a patio area, and they hosts numerous special events. Not shown on Mapa Map A

Dane Cellars – Sonoma Valley South of Sonoma Plaza – Wines: Chenin Blanc, Zinfandel, Cabernet Sauvignon – P.O. Box 555 - Vineburg CA. 95487 – www.danecellars.com – (707)–529-5856 – Hours: Appointment – bart@danecellars.com – This is a very small family winery producing excellent wines from an industry veteran. Not shown on map.

David Coffaro Vineyard and Winery – Dry Creek Valley – Intimate and Innovative – Wines: Pinot Noir, Cabernet Sauvignon, Petite Syrah, Carignane, Zinfandel, Estate Cuvee – 7485 Dry Creek Rd. Geyserville CA 95441 – www.coffaro.com – (707) 433-9715 – Hours: 11:00am–4:00pm – This is a family run winery by a long time local producer. You taste in the barrel room. They were one of the first producers locally to offer futures for sale. Map J

Davis Family Vineyards – Healdsburg at Front Street – Wines: Chardonnay, Syrah, Zinfandel, Cabernet Sauvignon, Pinot Noir, Apple Brandy, Olive Oil – 52 Front Street, Healdsburg CA 95448 – www.davisfamilyvineyards.com – (707) 433-3858 – Hours: 11:00am–4:00pm Thursday – Sunday – This winery produces a wide variety of wines, both from their own ridge top vineyards in the Russian River Valley, and from grapes sourced in the area, most notably Dutton Estates, a collection of vineyards spread around the southern side of the river. While they have a fair number of their own Zinfandel vines planted in the late 1800's, it is their younger Pinot and Syrah that standout and win the gold medals. The tasting/barrel room is one of the longest lasting Front Street Wineries in an eclectic commercial area beside the Russian River. It is charming experience and they have an outdoor patio next to the flowing water. Map F

De La Montanya – Dry Creek – Wines: Diverse – 999 Foreman Lane Healdsburg CA 95448 – www.dlmwine.com – (707) 433-3711 – Hours: 11:00am–4:30pm – This is a good winery with a fun approach. They are a little tricky to find because the turn off West Dry Creek Road onto Foreman Lane snakes around and goes under the road to get to the winery. They have a small tasting room and pretty grounds and they do nice events, but they have limited hours. Map K

De Loach Vineyards – Southern Russian River on Olivet Lane – Wines: Sauvignon Blanc, Chardonnay, Pinot Noir, Zinfandel – 1791 Olivet Rd. Santa Rosa CA 95401 – www.deloachvineyards.com – (707) 526-9111 – Hours: 10:00am–4:30pm – Appointments strongly suggested – This is the largest of the Olivet Lane wineries. They are Biodynamic/Organic and have a cool education demonstration garden. The tasting is in a separate hospitality house behind the winery with a large patio area and very comfortable indoor seating. It makes you feel like you are inside of a beautifully decorated private home. There is a separate picnic area. They make great wines that they offer in a gracious setting. Map J

De Lorimier Winery – Alexander Valley making Big Reds – Wines: Meritage, Malbec, Chardonnay, Sauvignon Blanc and Zinfandel – 2001 Highway. 128 Geyserville CA 95441 – www.delorimierwinery.com – (707) 857–2000 – Hours: 10:30am – 5:00pm – Owned by the Wilsons, who have numerous wineries in northern Sonoma, they are focusing on single vineyard designated Cabernets. Their vineyards also provide grapes for their various other wines. Map O

Deerfield Ranch Winery – Sonoma Valley Cave Tasting – Wines: Blends, Meritage, Cab, Chardonnay, Dessert Wine, Merlot, Pinot Noir, Sangiovese, Sauvignon Blanc, Syrah – 10200 Sonoma Highway Kenwood CA 95442 – www.deerfieldranch.com – (707) 833-5215 – Hours: 10:30-4:30pm They had a long road making their winery accessible to the public due to county regulations, but some wonderful wines come out of their caves. This is a high quality organic winery obsessed with clean, healthy wines that they pour in their charming caves. To reach the tasting area, you walk through their outside winery, jammed packed with tanks, sorters and presses, and the whole experience is remarkable. Map D

Deux Amis Winery see Zouzounis Wines

D and L Carinalli Vineyards – Sebastopol – Wines: Chardonnay, Pinot Noir, Pinot Grigio and Vin Rosé wines – 2900 Llano Road Santa Rosa, CA 95407 – www.dlcarinallivineyards.com – (707) 795-7052 – Hours: Appointment – A very small, but excellent family winery with no tasting room, but willing to do tastings by appointment. Not shown on Map

Donum Estate – Los Carneros Sculpture Park and Winery – Wines: Pinot Noir, Chardonnay, Rose – 24500 Ramal Road Sonoma, CA 95476 – www.thedonumestate.com – (707) 939-2290 – Hours: 10:00am–5:00pm Appointment – This very fine producer was transformed in order to host impressive modern sculpture from the owner's collection. The wines are excellent, and the sculpture tour is wonderful. The location on the rolling hills of Los Carneros can be cool early in the day and windy and sun soaked later, so dress accordingly for the tour, although the tasting is in their very unique tasting building. Map B

DRNK Wines – Southern Russian River – Chardonnay, Pinot Noir, Zinfandel – 3637 Frei Rd, Sebastopol, CA 95472 – www.drnkwines.com – (707) 823-3637 – Hours: 11-5 by Appointment - Closed Wednesdays – A cave winery dug in 1994, which you can see in their tour. They sell properly priced wines and offer a lovely experience. Ryan Kunde, the winemaker, is part of the Kunde family of Sonoma Valley. The winery was founded by Ryan and Katie, his wife in 2011– Map I

Dry Creek Vineyard – At the Center of the Valley – A Fun Experience – Wines: Chenin Blanc, Fumé Blanc, Zinfandel, Merlot, Cabernet Sauvignon, Meritage – 3770 Lambert Bridge Rd. Healdsburg CA 95448 – www.drycreekvineyard.com – (707) 433-1000 – Hours: 10:30am to 4:30pm – They are located near the Dry Creek Store and across from Passalacqua. Their photo gallery shows many of the celebrity events at which their wines have been poured. Not bad for an up–valley winery! They were one of the first modern wineries in the area and they continue to produce wonderful products. They have a nice picnic area shielded from the road, and the staff is friendly and relaxed. There is a small gift area and they do neat events. Map J

Dunstan Wines – Sonoma Valley West of the Plaza – Wines: Rose, Pinot Noir, Chardonnay – 1945 Felder Road Sonoma, CA 95476 – www.dunstanwines.com – (707) 933-3839 Hours: 10:00am to 3:00pm Wednesday – Sunday – Appointment – orders@dunstanwines.com – The Durell Vineyards sit on the western hills abeam downtown Sonoma. This is a premium producer that appeals to collectors that also sources grapes from Mendocino. Map A

Dutcher Crossing Winery – Dry Creek Valley – Charming and Relaxed – Wines: Zinfandel, Chardonnay, Cabernet Sauvignon, Merlot, Port, Petite Syrah, Sauvignon Blanc – 8533 Dry Creek Rd. Healdsburg CA 95448 – www.dutchercrossingwinery.com – (707) 431-2700 Hours: 11:00am–5:00pm – This is a small, family winery that is charming and popular. The tasting room is tiny and the winery is petite, but they produce some lovely wines often poured by the owners. Map L

Dutton Goldfield – Southwest Russian River Valley Tasting Room – Wines: Chardonnay, Pinot Noir, Syrah, Gewürztraminer, Zinfandel – 3100 Gravenstein Highway North, Sebastopol, CA 95472 – www.duttongoldfield.com – (707) 827-3600 – Hours 10:00am –4:30pm – The Dutton vineyards are highly respected for the quality of the wines they produce. Map I

Ektimo Vineyards – Southwest Russian River Valley – Wines: Chardonnay, Ektimo Brut, Zinfandel, Rose of Pinot Noir, Merlot – 4950 Ross Road Sebastopol, CA 95472 – www.ektimowines.com – (707) 827-3008 – Hours: Appointment – A surprisingly good winery in an older industrial building. Map I

Emeritus Vineyards – Southwest Russian River Valley – Wines: Bordeaux and Burgundy Blends – 2500 Gravenstein Highway N, Sebastopol, CA 95472 – www.emeritusvineyards.com– 707-823-9463 Hours: 10:30am to 4:00pm – They are in a modern building by the side of the road in a winery packed part of the valley. Map I

Emmitt-Scorsone – Dry Creek Valley –Cab Sauv, Merlot, Grenach, Barbera and various Italian Varietals – 1830 Jameson Rd, Healdsburg, CA 95448 – www.emmittscorsone.com – (707) 933-7603 – Hours: Appointment - Small family winery – Map J

En Garde Winery – Sonoma Valley – Wines: Cabernet Sauvignon, Pinot Noir – Their location is changing, but expect that their tastings will be at a location along Sonoma Highway, Kenwood, CA 95452 – www.engardewinery.com – (707) 282-9216. Not shown on Map

Enkidu Wine – Sonoma Eighth Street Wineries Corporate Park – Wines: Sauvignon Blanc, Syrah, Petite Syrah, Rhone Blends, Zinfandel, Pinot Noir, Cabernet Sauvignon – 21481 8th St. East Unit #1 Sonoma, CA 95476 – www.enkiduwines.com – (707) 939-3930 Hours: Appointment – They source fruit from Sonoma, Napa and Lake Counties. Map A

Eric Ross Winery – Glenn Ellen Tasting Room – Wines: Viognier, Chardonnay, Pinot Noir, Carignane, Zinfandel, Syrah, Zinfandel–Syrah Port, Marsanne–Rousanne, Port – 14300 Arnold Dr. Glen Ellen CA 95442 – www.ericross.com – (707) 939-8525 – Hours: 11:30–6:00pm Wednesday – Sunday. Map D

Enriquez Estate – Southern Russian River – Dry Muscat, tempranillo, Cabernet Franc, Pinot Noir, the Brisa Blend – 5960 Eastside Rd, Forestville, CA 95436 | Phone: www.enriquezwines.com – 707.347.9719 – Hours – They do private tastings at specific times and it can be accompanied by a gourmet lunch – Map I

F. Teldeschi Winery – Dry Creek Valley – Four Generations – Wines: Zinfandel, Port, Pink Zinfandel, Petite Syrah – 3555 Dry Creek Rd. Healdsburg CA 95448 – www.teldeschi.com – (707) 433-6626 – Hours: 12:00pm–5:00pm – There is so much wonderful history related to both Italy and Dry Creek Valley here that the family story alone is enough to bring you through the door. Most of their vineyards are planted to

Zinfandel, including many old vines, although they have a wide variety of grapes on their land. They always believed in the potential of Zinfandel and boy were they right! Dry Creek Zinfandel is practically the standard against which all else is measured. For many years, they sold their grapes to other wineries, including the famous Zinfandel of Ravenswood. Then the next generation took the plunge and started their own winery. The two Teldeschi brothers, John and Dan, create the wine from vineyard to bottle. They are conveniently located at the intersection of Dry Creek Road and Lytton Springs Road. They claim to be one hundred paces from the Dry Creek General Store, but they must have long legs. But that is a great place to get lunch. The tasting room is bright and friendly. We would suggest that you visit here earlier in the day because the front of the tasting room is glass and faces west, so late in the day it gets pretty bright in there. Map J

Fathia Vineyards – Kenwood Tasting Room – Wines: Pinot Noir, Moscato, Cabernet Sauvignon, Sauvignon Blanc – 8910 Sonoma Highway, Kenwood, CA 95452 – www.fathiawines.com 707-363-4859– Hours: Appointment – info@fathiawines.com – Optional Pairing – Add a small plate of delightful cheeses to enhance your flight. Not shown on Map

Ferrari-Carano Vineyards and Winery – Dry Creek Valley's Crown Jewel – Wines: Fumé Blanc, Zinfandel, Merlot, Malbec, Bordeaux blend, Grenache Rose, Dessert wines: Eldorado Gold (Semillon/Sauv blend) and Eldorado Noir (Black Muscat grape) – 8761 Dry Creek Rd. Healdsburg CA 95448 – www.ferrari-carano.com – (800) 831-0381 Hours: 10:00am – 5:00pm – This is Dry Creek's largest winery. Don't miss the gardens hidden behind the wall to the right as you approach. Go downstairs to the Enoteca and see the barrel caves that stretch between the tasting room and the winery. The Japanese style winery was built first, and then later, the Italianate–style visitor's center. They have a separate winery for the reds and the whites. In the Enoteca, rather than pour their reserve wines, they offer wines that are made in small lots, often two and three hundred cases. It is a wonderful experience. The only problem is that it doesn't have the great views of the tasting room upstairs. Map L

Fisher Vineyards – In the hills between Santa Rosa and St. Helena, on top of a hill, and in Calistoga – Wines: Cabernet Sauvignon, Cabernet Franc, Syrah, Chardonnay – 6200 St Helena Road Santa Rosa, CA 95404 – (707) 539-7511 – Hours: Appointment – www.fishervineyards.com – This is a small, boutique winery. The original winery is up the narrow winding road that turns into Spring Mountain Road, leading down into Napa. The house sits at the top of a narrow driveway. They also have vineyards and a winery on their property in Northern Napa. Not shown on Map

Flambeaux – Dry Creek Valley – Chardonnay, Rose', Zinfandel – 1333 Jack Pine Rd, Healdsburg, CA 95448 – website – (707) 637-9019 – Hours: 10-4 Appointment - Small family winery, High end producer – Map K

Flanagan Wines – Southern Dry Creek Valley – Wines: Chardonnay, Pinot Noir, Cabernet Sauvignon, Viognier, Merlot, Syrah – 435 W Dry Creek Road Healdsburg, CA 95448 – Hours: 10:00am to 5:00pm – Appointment – www.flanaganwines.com – This is a lovely winery at the south end of the Dry Creek Valley, close to the border of Russian River Valley. But their location does not reflect their wines since they have vineyards in Bennett Valley and the Petaluma Gap, among other places. They also purchase grapes. Map K

Flowers Winery – Russian River Valley – Wines: Pinot Noir, Chardonnay, Rosé – 4035 Westside Road Healdsburg, CA 95448 – www.flowerswinery.com – 707-723-4800 – Hours: Appointment – www.flowerswinery.com – reservations@flowerswinery.com – This is a long-time, highly respected producer of Pinot, going back to when the varietal was rarely planted. In recent years it was purchased by Quintessa of Napa, who subsequently purchased this great property on Westside Road, south of Healdsburg, which they renovated and expanded, before moving Flowers there. It is an elegant tasting now, and in demand so make your appointments early. At the time when Flowers first became well known they stood far above the small number of other Pinot producers, a very finicky grape. But today, there are numerous premium and ultra-premium wineries in the area at that level. Still, it is well worth the visit. Map H

Fog Crest Vineyard – Southern Russian River – Wines: Pinot Noir, Chardonnay, Rosé – 7606 Occidental Road Sebastopol, CA 95472 www.fogcrestvineyard.com – (707) 829-2006 – Hours: 11:00am–5:00pm – Appointment – www.fogcrestvineyard.com – This is a small, charming family winery that is perched on the top of a hill with great views. Map I

Foppiano Vineyards – Just south of Downtown Healdsburg known for their Petite Sirah – Wines: Zinfandel, Merlot,

Chardonnay, Sangiovese, Cabernet Sauvignon, Pinot Noir, Petite Sirah, White Zinfandel – 12707 Old Redwood Highway Healdsburg CA 95448 – www.foppiano.com – (707) 433-7272 Hours: 10:00am to 4:30pm – Self guided tour – This is one of the older wineries from this area that still consistently produces a good product. While the outside looks like farm buildings, they have a charming tasting room with a nice staff, pretty views of the vineyards and a nice gift selection. Next to the tasting room is a cute caboose. Map G

Fort Ross Vineyard, Winery – On the Sonoma Coast North of the Russian River – Wines: Chardonnay, Pinot Noir – 15725 Meyers Grade Road Jenner, CA 95450 – (707) 847-3460 – www.fortrossvineyard.com – Hours: Appointment – This beautiful winery sits on the hills overlooking the Pacific Ocean a short distance north of where the Russian River empties in the ocean, and a little south of the historic Fort Ross, Russia's last outpost in California. Winery wise, they have this area to themselves, so to deal with the fact that visitors have made them the destination, they offer wonderful food pairings to go with their wines. That bright sun and cool ocean breezes produce vineyards in this area that produce some of America's best Pinot Noir and Chardonnay. But, the area also comes with its hazards that make grape growing here challenging, birds, winds and fog. Not shown on Map

Francis Ford Coppola Winery – Alexander Valley – Family Friendly – Wines: Chardonnay, Pinot Noir, Syrah, Viognier, Cabernet Sauvignon, Zinfandel, Claret, Merlot, Malbec, Syrah–Shiraz, Pinot Grigio, Blanc de Blanc Sparkling wine, Rosé – 300 Via Archimedes Geyserville CA 95448 – www.franciscoppolawinery.com – (707) 857-1400 – Hours: 10:00am–5:00pm – This expansive property went through several owners including Coppola, who placed his medium range labels here, separating it from his Inglenook label in Napa. He since sold FFC to the family owned Delicato winery. It is a destination suitable for families to visit with a restaurant that expands onto large patios which is surrounded by some of its vineyards. There is a pool with cabanas and another bar style restaurant there. There are tasting bars downstairs and upstairs. The most exceptional attraction is the large collection of movie props from the director's career which are found throughout. In the busy season if you want to eat at the restaurant make reservations. Map O

Freeman Caves – Southern Russian River – Pinot Noir, Chardonnay, Riesling – 1300 Montgomery Road, Sebastopol, CA

95472 – www.freemanwinery.com - (707) 823-6937 – Hours: 10-5 by Appointment – One of the earliest pioneers in cool weather Pinot starting in the mid 1980's. Beautiful location amid the redwood trees. – Map I

Freestone Vineyards – Owned by the Joseph Phelps winery, this tasting room has been closed.

Frick Winery – Edge of Dry Creek Valley and Alexander Valley – Tucked Away – Wines: Syrah, Viognier, Cinsault, Grenache, Counoise, Grenache Blanc and Merlot – 23072 Walling Rd. Geyserville CA 95441 – www.frickwinery.com – (707) 857-1980 – Hours: 12–4:30 Saturday and Sunday – This is a small winery tucked away in the eastern hillsides of the Dry Creek Valley. They have limited hours, but the wines are hand made by the owner, and they focus on the Rhone varietals, which are not common in this area, so they are a nice change of pace. The tasting is in a charming, little cottage, that cannot handle a lot of people, and the parking lot is only suitable for about five cars. The views are beautiful. Map L

Fritz Underground Winery – Tasting in the Cave at the northern Edge of Dry Creek Valley – Wines: Chardonnay, Pinot Noir, Zinfandel, Cabernet Sauvignon, Sauvignon Blanc – 24691 Dutcher Creek Rd. Cloverdale CA 95425 – www.fritzwinery.com – (707) 894-3389 – Hours: 10:30am–4:30pm – The winery was started in 1979 and they reduced their quantity in favor of quality sourcing grapes from Russian River and Dry Creek. The gravity winery is entirely inside the cave. The wines are nicely priced and the chance to visit a hillside cave winery is not that common in this part of Sonoma. This is very much a family run operation that is looking to the future. They are fairly far north in the valley, but worth the ride. Map L

Furthermore Winery – Southern Russian River Valley – Wines: Chardonnay, Pinot Noir – 3541 Gravenstein Highway N, Sebastopol, CA 95472 – www.furthermorewines.com – (707) 823-3040 – Hours: 10:00am to 4:30pm – Map A

Garden Creek Ranch and Vineyard – Alexander Valley – Wines: Bordeaux and Burgundy – 2335 Geysers Rd, Geyserville, CA 95441 – www.gardencreekvineyards.com – (707) 433-8345 – Hours: Appointment – This is a small family winery run by a couple who grew up in the area. It is a totally authentic, charming experience and the wines are wonderful. Map I

Gary Farrell Vineyards and Winery – Russian River Valley North of the River – Great Location – Wines: Chardonnay, Pinot Noir, Zinfandel, Merlot, Cabernet Sauvignon, Blends – 10701 Westside Rd. Healdsburg CA 95448 – www.garyfarrellwines.com – (707) 473-2900 – Hours: 11:00am–4:00pm
The winery is up a long, steep driveway on a hill overlooking the Russian River Valley below. The tasting room is in a modern building that enjoys wonderful views to the south. They are ten minutes off River Road, over some winding roads, but it is a pretty ride, and it is a place that you will remember. Navigation: Reach them from River Road onto Wohler Road. Look for the pole with all the winery signs on it. At the Y in the road, by the Bed and Breakfast on the hill, bear left. Follow that over the one lane bridge, and then at the intersection of Westside Road turn left. The very steep winery drive will be on the right side. Map H

Glenlyon Vineyards and Winery – Sonoma Valley to Bennett Valley – Wines: Rose, Syrah, Rouge – 2750 John Hill Road Glen Ellen, CA 95442 – www.glenlyonwinery.com – (707) 484-0077 - Hours: Appointment – Squire@GlenLyonWinery.com – This is a charming family winery moving into its second generation on the hills of the Bennett Valley to the west of Glen Ellen. They are well-known for their Syrah but all the wines are good. The winery tour and tasting with the owner is exceptional, but plan to buy when you visit because the wines are that good. Map D

Gloria Ferrer Caves and Vineyards – Los Carneros – Sparkling Wines and Great Location – Wines: Sparkling, Blanc de Blancs, Brut, Blanc de Noirs, Cuvee, Brut Rosé, Chardonnay, Pinot Noir, Syrah – 23555 Carneros Highway. 121 Sonoma CA 95476 – www.gloriaferrer.com – (707) 996-7256 – Hours: 10:00am–5:00pm – They produce sparklers and their tasting room patio is a great place to enjoy them. They are more of a bar than a tasting room, but with the views and location who cares. Being in Los Carneros, they make a great first or last stop on a trip up from the city. They are owned by a large Spanish winery so they don't have a family winery feel, however, they've been in Sonoma long enough to absorb that wonderful hospitality that is famous here. Map A

Gopfrich – Dry Creek Valley – Wines: Cabernet Sauvignon, Zinfandel, Syrah – 7462 W. Dry Creek Rd. Healdsburg CA 95448 – www.gopfrich.com – (707) 433-1645 – Hours: Appointment – This is a small production, family run estate located in the north western part of the Dry Creek Valley. The wines are only available there and the tastings are by appointment. Map J

Gordenker – Sonoma Valley – Wines: Sauvignon Blanc, Pinot Noir, Cabernet Sauvignon, Rose – Tasting Room – 12201 CA–12, Glen Ellen, CA 95442 – (707) 934-7759 – Hours: Appointment – michele@gordenker.com – This is a small family vineyard started in 1946. Not shown on Map

Graton Ridge Winery – South Russian River Valley – Charming Small Tasting Room – Wines: Sauvignon Blanc, Chardonnay, Rose, Zinfandel, Pinot Noir, Cabernet Sauvignon, Zinfandel Port, Apple Port – 3561 Gravenstein Highway N. Sebastopol, CA 95472 – www.gratonridge.com – (707) 823-3040 – Hours: 10:00am–4:30pm Friday–Monday – This is a cute little place with a great staff and lovely wines that sits amid the apple groves along the Gravenstein Highway. From the outside, it seems low key, but inside it is a charming experience with a comfortable bar, and some pretty features, murals and lovely gift items. Map I

Gundlach Bundschu Winery – Sonoma Valley – The Rhinefarm – Wines: Zinfandel, Gewürztraminer, Chardonnay, Pinot Noir, Cabernet Franc, Merlot, Cabernet Sauvignon – 2000 Denmark St. Sonoma CA 95448 – www.gunbun.com – (707) 938-3015 – Hours: 11:00am–4:00pm – Located minutes from the Sonoma Plaza and started as a farm in 1858, it is still in the same family. This is the southern edge of the Sonoma Valley, near Los Carneros so these are good food wines, typical of that cool climate. They have a nice picnic patio with a pretty view, and a short cave tour. There are hiking trails nearby but watch out for the rattlesnakes. Map A

Gustafson Family Vineyard – Northern Tip of Dry Creek Valley 9100 Skaggs Springs Road, Geyserville – www.gfvineyard.com – (707) 433-2371 – Hours: 10:00am to 6:00pm – Appointment – Picnic Area – This family vineyard and winery is at the northern edge of the Dry Creek Valley, just south of Lake Sonoma and past Ferrari Carano and Sbragia family. So you need to be heading there, because there are no other wineries nearby, but it is a great place to grow grapes. Map L

Hamel Family Wines – Sonoma Valley – Wines: Zinfandel, Sauvignon Blanc, Rose – 15401 Sonoma Highway, Sonoma, CA 95476 (707)–996-5800 – Hours: 10:00am to 5:00pm Appointment – www.hamelfamilywines.com – This is a beautiful, biodynamic winery a short ride north of the Plaza. The tasting includes a tour of the winery. The hospitality building is modern and elegant with great views. These slopes had been farmed for a long time by one of the local Italian American families before the Hamel family purchased it. Map D

Hanna Winery – Alexander Valley with Great Views – Wines: Merlot, Zinfandel, Pinot Noir, Cabernet Sauvignon, Sauvignon Blanc, Syrah, Blends, Cabernet Franc, Rosé – 9280 Highway 128 Healdsburg CA 95448 – www.hannawinery.com – (707) 575-3371 – Hours: 10:00am–5:00pm – This winery is located at the lower edge of the Alexander Valley in a spectacular location with great views of the valley and the distant hills. They make big reds with lots of depth and softness. They have a charming building with a pleasant staff. When you are coming to Alexander Valley from Napa (Calistoga) via Knight's Valley on Route 128, this makes a nice first stop. Map N

Hanna Winery – Southern Russian River Valley – Wines: Merlot, Zinfandel, Pinot Noir, Cabernet Sauvignon, Sauvignon Blanc, Syrah, Blends, Cabernet Franc, Rosé – 5353 Occidental Rd Santa Rosa CA 95401 – www.hannawinery.com – (707) 575-3371 – Hours: 10:00am–4:00pm – These are the Russian River vineyards and tasting room connected with the Alexander Valley winery. It is a charming tasting room and the wines are good. They are near Balleto, Dutton Goldfield, Lynmar and Graton Ridge. Map I

Hanzell Vineyards – Sonoma Valley – Historic Pinot Noir – Wines: Chardonnay, Pinot Noir – 18596 Lomita Ave. Sonoma CA 95476 – www.hanzell.com – (707) 996-3860 – Hours: Appointment – These are among California's oldest Pinot Noir and Chardonnay vineyards, which are planted on hillsides, and can be seen from downtown Sonoma. They include a significant portion of the original vines, so the production is small, about one ton per acre, although some replanting has been done recently. They do their tastings by appointment, but allow extra time to get there because they are reached via a winding, climbing gravel road, but they are worth the effort. They do a vineyard, cave and winery tour and a sit-down tasting in a great old building patterned on a classic French winemaking building. They also do a true reserve selection from their extensive collection. The tastings are expensive by Sonoma standards, but for the serious aficionado it is worth the price. The tour and tasting is not rushed so plan on spending a couple of hours there. They have spectacular views of Sonoma and the southern valley. Map D

Hartford Family Winery – Russian River Valley – Lovely Wines from Green Valley – Wines: Pinot Noir, Chardonnay, Zinfandel – 8075 Martinelli Rd. Forestville CA 95436 – www.hartfordwines.com – (707) 887-8010 – Hours: 10:00am–4:30pm – They are located on a side road that stretches between River Road and Gravenstein Highway. They make some nice wines in a pretty location. The building has some of the classic, French style architecture that you see at Kendall Jackson. Map I

Harvest Moon Estate – Russian River Valley – A Little Jewel of a Winery – Wines: Zinfandel, Gewürztraminer, Sparkling Gewürztraminer, Pinot Noir – 2192 Olivet Rd. Santa Rosa CA 95401 – www.harvestmoonwinery.com – (707) 573-8711 – Hours: 10:30am–5:00pm – This is a charming, small winery, with a pretty building, that makes lovely wines. It is one of the Olivet Road wineries, so the vineyards produce dependable and enjoyable flavors. The tasting is low-key and friendly, and they do great events. Map I

Hawkes Wines – Alexander Valley Tasting Room – Wines: Chardonnay, Merlot, Cabernet Sauvignon – 6734 Highway 128 Healdsburg CA 95448 – www.hawkeswine.com – (707) 433-4295 – Hours: 10:00am–5:00pm The Hawkes family has been growing grapes for quite a while in Alexander Valley and they have some wonderful vineyards up on the hillsides to the east of their tasting room. Great grapes make great wines. The staff is gracious and quite knowledgeable, and the tasting room is roomy and nicely appointed. Map M

Hawley Wines – Downtown Healdsburg Tasting Room – Wines: Wide Variety – 36 North St Healdsburg CA 95448 – www.hawleywine.com – (707) 473-9500 – Hours: 11:00am–6:00pm – This tasting room is just steps from the Healdsburg plaza. They make fine, moderately priced wines, and they have a good staff. Their wines come from their own organic hillside vineyards overlooking the Dry Creek Valley. They make a wide variety. Not shown on Map

Holdredge Wines – Downtown Healdsburg – Wines: Pinot Noir – 51 Front St. Healdsburg CA 95448 – www.holdredge.com – (707) 431-1424 – Hours: 11:00am–4:30pm Saturday – Sunday – This small winery handcrafts Russian River Pinot Noir. They have limited tasting room hours and only make about 3,000 cases. However, they are conveniently located nearby other tasting rooms, so when you go touring in Healdsburg on the weekend, check them out. Not shown on Map

Homewood Winery – Los Carneros – Authentic Handmade – Wines: Sauvignon Blanc, Chardonnay, Pinot Noir, Grenache, Merlot, Syrah, Zinfandel, Blends – 23120 Burndale Rd. Vineburg CA 95487 – www.homewoodwinery.com – (707) 996-6353 – Hours: 10:00am-4:00pm – This is a completely authentic Sonoma winery, with the tanks just on the other side of the wall from the tasting bar. The winemaker and owner is David Homewood and he is often on hand to chat about the wines, which are good. In the warmer weather, the tastings are done outside on the picnic tables. Although the winery is located in the Los Carneros district, David buys his grapes from various sources, including Napa so he can pick and choose the best. They are located just off Highways 121/12. Map A

Hook and Ladder Winery – Russian River – Olivet Rd – Wines: Cabernet Sauvignon, Zinfandel, White Zinfandel, Pinot Noir, Chardonnay, Gewürztraminer, Rosé – 2134 Olivet Rd. Santa Rosa CA 95401 – www.hookandladderwinery.com – (707) 526-2255 – Hours: 10:00am-4:30pm – This is a small winery that makes some wonderful wines and offers them in a casual setting with the tanks and barrels in site of the tasting bar. The walls are decorated with Firehouse emblems and if you show your card as a volunteer or full-time fireman tastings are free. An Olivet Road gem. Map I

Hop Kiln Winery – Russian River Valley – Architectural Destination – Wines: Cabernet Sauvignon, Chardonnay, Riesling, Zinfandel – 6050 Westside Rd. Healdsburg CA 95448 – www.hopkilnwinery.com – (707) 433-6491 – Hours: 10:00am-5:00pm – They are located halfway up Westside Road in a beautifully restored Hop Kiln from years past when this was an important hop growing area. There are pictures along the walls showing the fascinating history of the place. They have a great gift area including lots of foods, snacks and chocolate. They make good value wines including some unusual blends, poured by a friendly staff. This is a nice place for a picnic and a great place to stop later in the day when some of your party might be more interested in shopping than tasting. They are owned by Landmark Vineyards and are referred to as Landmark at Hop Kiln. Map H

Idell Family Vineyards – Sonoma Valley – Wines: Chardonnay, Syrah Zinfandel – 18900 Carriger Road Sonoma CA – (707) 938-7765 – Appointment – www.idellfamilyvineyards.com – An interesting family winery west of downtown Sonoma. Not shown on Map

Imagery Estate Winery – Sonoma Valley – Art Lover Destination – Wines: Cabernet Franc, Petite Syrah, Barbera, Sangiovese, Malbec, White Burgundy, Pinot Blanc, Viognier, Port – 14335 Highway 12 Glen Ellen CA 95442 – www.imagerywinery.com – (877) 550-4278 – Hours: 10:00am–5:00pm – This place is a jewel, pouring small lot wines that include many unusual varietals only sold at the winery. After commissioning art for labels for many years, they created the world's largest collection of art created expressly for labels, which was donated to Sonoma State University by the family. But the new owners have continued the label tradition and those painting are displayed in the tasting room. The staff will share the story with you, and the book cataloging the collection is often on the bar. This is connected to the Benziger Family Winery and they will often give you a coupon for a tasting there. They have picnic tables, bocce courts, a nice gift area with unique items related to their labels, and extensive picnic areas. Navigation: They share a driveway with the Arrowood Winery. As you come north from the Sonoma Plaza, after you pass the B.R. Cohn winery on the left–hand side, their driveway will come up on the right side just past the curve. Look for the banners. Map D

Inman Family – Russian River Valley Olivet Road – Wines: Rose, Pinot Noir, Sparkling, Chardonnay – 3900 Piner Road Santa Rosa, CA 95401 – www.inmanfamilywines.com – (707) 293–9576 – Hours: 11:00am–5:00pm – Appointment – this is a lovely little winery with wonderful wines made in small lots by the owner, Kathleen Inman. Map H

Iron Horse Vineyards – Russian River Valley – Great Views – Wines: Chardonnay, Pinot Noir, Viognier, Sangiovese, Merlot, Cabernet Sauvignon, Multiple Sparkling Wines – 9786 Ross Station Rd. Sebastopol CA 95472 – www.ironhorsevineyards.com – (707) 887-1507 Hours: 11:00am–3:30pm – This is a pet friendly, beautiful location, situated down a narrow road. The tasting is outside under a lean–to, looking east out over the hills. The staff is friendly, the wines are great, and the experience is not to be missed. Get there early in the day when you can enjoy the morning sunshine, they open at 11 and they close early. Their wines tend to be lighter and it makes them a good first stop in the Russian River Valley. They are in wide distribution, but there you will taste their small production wines that are only available at the winery. Map I

J Vineyards and Winery – Russian River Valley – Sparkling Wines and Great Pairings – Wines: Pinot Noir, Pinot Gris, Chardonnay, Vin Gris, Pear Liqueur, Rosé – 11447 Old Redwood Highway. Healdsburg CA 95448 – www.jwine.com – (707) 431-5430 – Hours: 11:00am–5:00pm – This is a wonderful sparkling and still wine producer that does great food pairings in an elegant setting. They share a driveway with Rodney Strong. They have a nice gift section and a friendly staff. This is a great place to end a day of tasting, which may explain why they get so busy late in the day. The place is a lot of fun. The food pairings are well known, and while you can sometimes arrange them on a walk in basis, it is better to set up an appointment. Map G

J. Rickards Winery – Alexander Valley – Wines: Sauvignon Blanc, Rose, Zinfandel, Syrah, Cabernet Sauvignon – 24505 Chianti Road Cloverdale, CA 95425 – www.jrwinery.com – (707) 758-3441 – Hours: 11:00am–5:00pm Monday – Saturday – info@jrwinery.com. – Map O

J. Rochioli Vineyards and Winery – Russian River Valley – A White House Wine – Wines: Sauvignon Blanc, Chardonnay, Pinot Noir – 6192 Westside Rd. Healdsburg CA 95448 www.rochioliwinery.com (707) 433-2305 – Hours: 11:00am–4:00pm – This is a small tasting room hidden away in the Russian River Valley. They can be tricky to spot sometimes, but they are located just south of the hard to miss Hop Kiln Winery, on the same side of the road. They produce great wines, but most of it goes to their wine club, so when you visit, the list they pour from may be small. Their wines have been poured at the White House for many years. This is a pretty place with great views of the vineyards along the river. Map H

Jacuzzi Family Vineyards – Los Carneros – Wines: Chardonnay, Pinot Noir, Barbera, Sangiovese, Arneis, Merlot, Nebbiolo, Primitivo, Pinot Grigio, Moscato Blanc – 24724 Arnold Dr. Sonoma CA 95476 – www.jacuzziwines.com – (707) 931-7575 – Hours: 10:00am–5:00pm – This Italian style winery is owned by Cline, across the road. They have a spacious tasting room, specializing in Italian varietals. The Olive Press shares the building where you can taste olive oil. Nice gift shops. There is something for everyone, wine lover and shopper. It is convenient to San Francisco via the Golden Gate Bridge. They make a great first or last stop on a tour originating in the city. The wines are very good, refreshing and well made. It has wonderful Italian style architecture, gardens and expansive event spaces. Map A

Jigar Wines – Forestville Tasting Room – Wines: Cabernet Sauvignon, Pinot Noir, Merlot, Chardonnay, Syrah – 6615 Front St, Forestville, CA 95436 – www.jigarwines.com – (707) 820-1225 – Hours: 11:00am–5:00pm. Not on Map

Jordan Vineyard and Winery – Alexander Valley – Famous Reds Wines: Cabernet Sauvignon, Chardonnay, Dessert Wine, Olive Oil – 1474 Alexander Valley Rd. Healdsburg CA 95448 www.jordanwinery.com – (707) 431-5250 – Hours: Appointment Tours Monday – Saturday Closed Sunday – This is a grand estate in the Alexander Valley, with a wonderful staff and well regarded Bordeaux–style wines. This tasting is for the serious wine lover, since the wines are expensive. They are by appointment with limited slots so plan well in advance. They do both tastings and tours at different times. The sign on Alexander Valley Road is small, but the driveway entrance is quite broad and well done. If you are coming from Healdsburg, it is on the right side. It looks like a French Chateau by intention. The big difference is that the Alexander Valley has nicer weather than Bordeaux. Map M

Joseph Jewell – Forestville Tasting Room – Wines: Pinot Noir, Chardonnay – 6542 Front St, Forestville, CA 95436 – www.josephjewell.com – (707) 820-1621 – Hours: 11:00am to 7:00pm Thursday – Monday, Closed Tuesday and Wednesday – info@josephjewell.com. Not shown on Map

Joseph Swan Vineyards – Russian River Valley – Rustic and Charming – Wines: Zinfandel, Pinot Noir, Syrah – 2916 Laguna Rd. Forestville CA 95436 – www.swanwinery.com – (707) 573-3747 – Hours: 11:00am–4:00pm Appointment. This long time, small, family winery is just off River Road with wonderful views of the vineyards. You walk past the bins and tanks to get to the tasting room, which doubles as the barrel room. They also taste outsidde on the patio. The whole experience is country and friendly and well worth the ride. The wines are good. Limited to groups of 8 or less. Map I

Kamen Estate - Downtown Sonoma –Wines: Syrah, Sauvignon Blanc, Cabernet Franc, Cabernet Sauvignon, – 111B East Napa Street Sonoma, California 95476 – www.kamenwines.com – 707-938-7292 – Hours: 12:00pm to 5:00pm. They have both a downtown tasting room and a mountain estate. If want to taste at the estate make an appointment, and then they drive to the estate property, which is way up in the very scenic hills. They are next to Maya Restaurant on Map C.

Keller Estate – Petaluma Over the Western Hills from Los Carneros A Unique Estate – Wines: Rosé, Chardonnay, Pinot Gris, Pinot Noir, Syrah – 5875 Lakeville Highway. Petaluma CA 95954 – www.kellerestate.com – (707) 765-2117 – Hours: 11:00am–4:00pm. Thursday – Sunday – This is an expansive vineyard and winery located off Highway 101 in Petaluma, which makes it convenient to San Francisco. The winemaking facility and the grounds and buildings are grand. They have a good tour and a nice art collection spread around the grounds. They are a bit off the beaten tour track but worth the effort. There is a race car track that runs through the property because the owners are big fans of the sport. Not shown on Map

Kendall-Jackson – Russian River Valley – A Famous Brand – Wines: Cabernet Sauvignon, Merlot, Syrah, Chardonnay, Pinot Noir, Riesling, Sauvignon Blanc, Zinfandel, Olive Oil – 5007 Fulton Rd. Fulton CA 95439 – www.kj.com – (707) 433-7102 – Hours: 10:00am – 5:00pm – This is essentially a very big tasting room surrounded by beautiful gardens and wonderful demonstration vineyard. You can see the French style building from Highway 101. They have a tasting bar and outdoor seating and it is a gracious experience. Map G

Kenwood Vineyards Winery – Sonoma Valley – Wines: Cabernet Sauvignon, Chardonnay, Sauvignon Blanc, Zinfandel, Pinot Noir, Merlot, Gewürztraminer – 9592 Sonoma Highway. Kenwood CA 95452 – www.kenwoodvineyards.com – (707) 833-5891 – Hours: 10:00am–4:30pm – They are located in the center of Kenwood Because the winery sits on a slight rise, it provides a pleasant view of the vines and the town of Kenwood. Their Jack London Vineyards from Sonoma Mountain wines stand out. Yes, the famous writer of Call of the Wild lived just up the road. Map D

Kinsella – Dry Creek Valley – Cabernet Sauvignon – French Rd, Healdsburg, CA 95448 – kinsellawines.com– 855-707-8686 – Hours: Appointment - Small family wineryfrom the Jersey Boys Vineyard, called that because it was the owners investment in the show that paid for the winery. Thomas River Brown is the winemaker – Map K

Kistler Estate – Southern Russian River – Chardonnay, Pinot Noir – 7095 Trenton-Healdsburg Rd, Forestville, CA 95436 – www.kistlervineyards.com – (707) 657-7665 – Hours: 9-5 by Appointment – They are one of the first of the region's premium Pinot producer. Their tasting is low key and geared to collectors. – Map G

Kivelstadt Cellars – Sonoma Valley - Carneros –Wines: Syrah, Sauvignon Blanc, Zinfandel , Pinot Noir – 22900 Broadway Sonoma, CA 95476 – www.kivelstadtcellars.com – (707) 938-7001 – Hours: 12:00pm to 5:00pm. Map B

Kobler Estate Winery – Russian River Valley – Wines: Sauvignon Blanc, Syrah, Rose , Chardonnay, Pinot Noir – 4630 Gravenstein Highway North, Sebastopol, California 95472 – www.koblerestatewinery.com – (707) 473-8287 – 11:00am–5:00pm – Appointment – info@koblerestatewinery.com. A small family winery with four acres plus of vineyards. Map I

Kokomo Wines – Dry Creek Valley at the Timber Crest Center – Wines: Sauvignon Blanc, Chardonnay, Pinot Noir, Zinfandel, Cabernet Sauvignon, Syrah, Petite Syrah – 4791 Dry Creek Road Healdsburg CA 95448 – www.kokomowines.com – (707) 433-0200 – Hours: 11:00am–4:30pm – This is a newer winery based on long term vineyards located just behind the property. The tasting room is also the winery, and the sense of being right where everything happens is fun. They make good wines and have a basic tasting room. Being located in the Timber Crest Center, they are walking distance to other good wineries so it creates a nice social scene, especially later in the day. Map J

Korbel Champagne Cellars – Russian River Valley – Historic Location – Wines: Sparkling and Still wines – 13250 River Rd. Guerneville CA 95446 – www.korbel.com – (707) 824-7000 – Hours: 10:00am–5:00pm (4:30 in Winter) – This is one of California's oldest sparkling wine houses, founded in 1882 by two Polish brothers. They are located on River Road, on the way to the Pacific Ocean, just outside of downtown Guerneville. The fog and cool air that flows in from the sea help to create conditions that suit Chardonnay and Pinot Noir perfectly. The tasting room is spacious with a nice gift area. Korbel's market is one of the best local places to stop for lunch with lots of seating outdoors among the redwood trees. Most people know the Korbel label as a modestly priced, sparkling wine, but when you visit here, you will taste and buy wines that are only sold at the winery. Between the lovely valley breezes, the history, frequent tours, architecture and deli, what's not to like? Map G

Kosta Browne Winery – Sebastopol at the Barlow Center – 200 Morris St, Sebastopol, CA 95472 – (707) 823-7430 – www.kostabrowne.com – Hours: Appointment for Wine Club Members This is a popular wine for collectors available through their wine club, and typically they have a waiting list. Their winery is located at the rear of the popular Barlow center in downtown Sebastopol, which is a great collection of restaurants, shops, galleries and tasting rooms. If you are touring in the southern part of the Russian River Valley including a visit to the Barlow center will give you some great insights about the local culture. G

Kunde Family Estate - Sonoma Valley – Five Generations Wines: Sauvignon Blanc, Chardonnay, Syrah, Zinfandel, Merlot, Cabernet Sauvignon, Primitivo, Sangiovese, Barbera, Gewürztraminer, Grenache Rosé, Meritage, Zinfandel Port – 9825 Sonoma Highway, Kenwood CA 95452 – www.kunde.com – (707) 833-5501 – Hours: 10:30–4:30 – The Kunde family farms their land in one of the most beautiful parts of the Valley of the Moon. Across the road is a charming restaurant in case you need a place for lunch. Besides a friendly tasting bar, Kunde offers a wonderful sit–down reserve tasting. They also do guided tours of their barrel caves, behind the winery under the beautifully terraced, vine covered hillsides. They also do tastings on top of the hill under the trees with views of the valley. For many years they sold a wide variety of grapes to other wineries, and then, in the early 1990's, they started making their own wine. As a result, they offer a wonderful variety and the wines are a great deal for the quality. The tasting room and winery building is based on a Georgian style cow barn that sat on the site for many years. They have picnic tables outside by the fountain, nice gifts, and a wonderful ambience. They are a great value and the place is a lot of fun. Bring a picnic and enjoy the view and the wines. Groups of 10 or more should call ahead. Map D

La Crema Estate at Saralee's Vineyard – Russian River Valley – Wines: Pinot Noir, Pinot Gris, Pinot Rose, Chardonnay, Syrah, Viognier – 3575 Slusser Rd. Windsor, CA 95492 – www.lacrema.com – (707) 431-9400 – Hours: 10:00am –5:30pm – This is a large winery for a well-known brand, located near the Sonoma Airport on the north side of River Road. The tasting is in an historic barn built in 1900. Map G

La Follette Wines – Poured at the Quivera Winery

Lago di Merlo Vineyard and Winery – Dry Creek Valley – Wines: Lago di Merlo, Chardonnay, Sangiovese, Rosato, Amanti II – 3495 Skagg's Spring Rd. Geyserville CA 95441 – www.lagodimerlo.com – (707)473-0146 – Hours: Appointment – They are located at the very top of Dry Creek Valley just south of Lake Sonoma so make an appointment before you go. Map L

Lambert Bridge Winery – A Dry Creek Jewel – Wines: Sauvignon Blanc, Chardonnay, Viognier, Zinfandel, Crane Creek Cuvée, Petite Syrah, Merlot, Cabernet Franc, Cabernet Sauvignon, oils and condiments – 4085 W. Dry Creek Rd. Healdsburg CA 95448 – www.lambertbridge.com – (707) 431-9600 – Hours: 10:30am–4:30pm Appointment – This is a beautiful, small winery, with a great picnic area, a nice gift collection, a knowledgeable and friendly staff, a great tasting room and spectacular wines. They run numerous events on their picnic grounds complete with an outdoor kitchen. They have both a basic and reserve tasting, and the best way to get their wines is through the wine club because their production is limited and the wines are popular. Many of their wines are distributed solely to their wine club. This area normally grows great grapes, so the variable becomes how much effort and labor the owners are willing to put into the farm work and winemaking. In Lambert Bridge's case, that means having three winemakers, state of the art equipment and a lot of money spent on new French oak barrels. This results in wines that compete well with Napa at Sonoma prices. Their seated pairing in the barrel room are very cool. Map J

Lancaster Estate Winery – Russian River Valley – At the southern edge of the Alexander Valley – An Ultra Premium Producer – Wines: Cabernet Sauvignon Blends, Sauvignon Blanc – 15001 Chalk Hill Rd. Healdsburg CA 95448 – www.lancaster-estate.com – (707) 433-8178 Hours: Tuesday – Saturday Appointment – This is a stunning, by appointment, smaller winery. The tastings are private and are conducted in the library room in their beautiful caves. They are located close to both the Chalk Hill and Knights Valley districts. Be serious when you make your appointment because there is a cancellation fee. This winery is for the enthusiast who likes big red wines in the Bordeaux style and who likes an exclusive experience. The staff is friendly and knowledgeable. The vineyards and winery are tucked into a lovely little valley. The fifty plus acres are planted to the classic Bordeaux red varietals. Even though they are technically in the Russian River Valley, they are more easily reached from Alexander Valley Road. While you can take Chalk Hill Road north to get there, past the Chalk Hill and Roth wineries, we don't recommend it because it is a narrow and winding road. Map N

Landmark Winery – Sonoma Valley – Wonderful Gardens – Wines: Chardonnay, Pinot Noir, Syrah and expanding each year in the Rhone Varietals – 101 Adobe Canyon Rd. Kenwood CA 95452 – www.landmarkwine.com (707) 833-0218 – Hours: 10:00am–4:30pm Appointment – This is lovely winery specializing in Burgundy and Rhone wines, The winery is built like a classic Spanish compound, with the buildings protecting an inner garden which is perfect for picnics and bocce. These are some of the prettiest and most comfortable winery grounds in wine country. The wines are excellent and have been served many times at the White House. A hidden treasure is the President's Tower tasting room where a private, seated tasting for eight can be scheduled. The walls are lined with White House menus from the past twenty years. The views from the tower tasting room take your breath away, including the expanse of the Valley of the Moon with Sugar Loaf Mountain and Hood Mountain in the distance. For such a low key, gracious winery, they produce a wonderful winery experience and of course, wonderful wines. You can see the winery from Highway 12, but you need to turn right on Adobe Canyon Road to reach the entrance. They are just north Chateau St. Jean. Map D

La Rochelle – Sonoma Valley – Wines: Pinot Noir, Chardonnay – 233 Adobe Canyon Road, Kenwood, CA 95452 – www.lrwine.com – (707) 302-8000 – Hours: 11:00am–5:00pm – Appointment – This is a charming family winery that produces wonderful Pinot Noir, as well as Chardonnay. It is very small and calling ahead for an appointment is a very good idea. They are located just past Landmark. Map D

Larson Family Winery – Los Carneros – Family Style – Wines: White and Red table wines, Chardonnay, Semi sweet Gewürztraminer, Cuveé Rosé, Pinot Noir Rosé, Pinot Noir, Merlot, Meritage, Petite Syrah, Cabernet Sauvignon, Pinot Grigio – 23355 Millerick Rd. Sonoma CA 95476 – www.LarsonFamilyWinery.com – (707) 938-3031 – Hours: 10:00am–5:00pm – This is as much a ranch as a winery and in all ways, a lot of fun for a family with kids. They have bocce, horses, and have a petting zoo with a picnic area and plenty of space for the kids to run around. This was the site of the Sonoma Rodeo and the pictures about its history are cool. The tasting room feels like a barn's tack room. Being a ranch, it is not as slick and polished as many of their neighboring wineries but well worth the visit. Map A

Lasseter Family Winery – Sonoma Valley – Beautiful seated tasting – Wines: A wide variety – 1 Vintage Lane Glen Ellen CA 95442 –www.lasseterfamilywinery.com – (707) 933-2800 – Hours: by Appointment – The winery of John and Nancy Lassiter. John is the head of Pixar and continues Sonoma's tradition of being a home to artists and animators. It is a pretty winery and a gracious tasting room. The art and style of the place is delightful. They do limited appointments, but they are easy to arrange and it is near Wellington and Loxton. Map D

Laurel Glen Vineyard – Downtown Glen Ellen Tasting Room – Wines: Cabernet Sauvignon, Rose, Sauvignon Blanc – 13750 Arnold Dr Suite #9, Glen Ellen, CA 95442 – www.laurelglen.com – Hours: Appointment. Grapes from Sonoma Mountain. They are in a lovely building across the street from the Glen Ellen market shown on Map D

Lauterbach Cellars – Russian River Valley – Wines: Syrah, Sparkling Pinot, Pinot Noir, Rose – 3420 Woolsey Road Windsor, CA 95492 – (707) 578-0537 – Hours: Appointment. They are not shown on the map but they are located just south of the Martinelli Winery which is on River Road, Map G

Ledson Winery and Vineyards – Sonoma Valley – Grand Tasting Room – Wines: A wide variety – 7335 Highway 12 Santa Rosa CA 95409 – www.ledsonwinery.com – (707) 537-3810 Hours: 10:00am to 5:00pm – This is known locally as the 'castle', but it was originally built as a home and then became a tasting room and event space. It has a deli, spacious, rather austere tasting rooms and picnic tables for their items. They offer a wide variety of wines. They are at the top of the Sonoma Valley where flattens around Santa Rosa, so it makes a good place to stop for a tasting before heading south again. Map D

Limerick Lane Cellars – Russian River Valley – Off the Beaten Path Wines: Zinfandel, Syrah, Pinot Noir, Cabernet Sauvignon – 1023 Limerick Lane Healdsburg CA 95448 – www.limericklanewines.com – (707) 433-9211 – Hours: 10:00am to 5:00pm – This is a friendly, small winery founded by three friends. They make good wines and have a nice staff. The bottle shaped swimming pool is cool, not to make too obvious a pun. They are tucked over on Limerick Lane, safely off the beaten track, but worth a visit. Map G

Little Vineyards – Sonoma Valley – Wines: Zinfandel, Cabernet Sauvignon, Syrah – 15188 Sonoma Highway, Glen

Ellen CA 95442 www.littlevineyards.com – (707) 996-2750 – Hours: 11:00am–5:00pm Thursday – Monday – This is a small, casual winery. The driveway is on the left–hand side (as you are heading north) just before the entrance for B.R. Cohn so it is convenient to the Sonoma Plaza. The tasting room/winery is surrounded by older vines. They have some outside seating in case you have packed a picnic. Map D

Littoral Wines – Russian River Valley – Wines: Chardonnays, Pinot Noirs – 788 Gold Ridge Road Sebastopol, CA 95472 – 707–823-9586 Hours: 9:00am to 5:00pm Monday – Sunday – littorai.com – This is a highly respected producer of Pinot Noir. The wine maker worked in France and the approach is biodynamic. The winery and vineyards are out of the way but they have an informative tour. They are in the lower left corner of Map G

Longboard Vineyards - Healdsburg – Surfer's Paradise – Wines: Syrah, Cabernet Sauvignon, Merlot – 5 Fitch St. Healdsburg CA 95448 www.longboardvineyards.com – (707) 433-3473 – Hours: 11:00am –7:00pm Thursday – Saturday, Sunday 11:00am–5:00pm – This is a tasting room and winery just a few minutes from the Healdsburg Plaza and nearby the Front Street Wineries. It was started by friends who share a love of surfing and the tasting room is decorated with surfboards and related photos. Map F

Loxton Cellars – Sonoma Valley – The Personal Touch – Wines: Rosé, Zinfandel, Syrah, Cabernet Sauvignon, Syrah Port, Chardonnay, Shiraz – 11466 Dunbar Rd. Glen Ellen CA 95442 – www.loxtoncellars.com – (707) 935-7221 – Hours: 11:00am–5:00pm – This is a small winery where Chris Loxton often pours for you and does the tours. You walk past the winemaking equipment to reach the barrel room/tasting room. They have picnic tables out front so bring a picnic. The entire staff is knowledgeable and friendly, partly because they don't just pour, they also make wine. Chris is from an Australian grape growing family, and a former physics professor, so his winemaking style is informed and unique. Visit during crush and you'll get your feet wet. No, you will not be stomping grapes, but the crush pad is in front of the building, so you are going to be walking through juice on the way to your tasting. The staff, including Chris, is almost always willing to chat about the process as they work. These are some great wines and they are only sold here! They also have one of the best Ports in the county. Chris has been doing a daily vineyard tour by appointment that is well worth taking. Map D

Lynmar Winery – Southern Russian River Valley – Wines: Pinot Noir, Chardonnay, Vin Gris, Syrah – 9060 Frei Rd. Sebastopol CA 95472 – www.lynmarwinery.com – (707) 829-3374 – Hours: 10:00am–5:00pm Appointment – This is a jewel of a winery tucked into a lovely hollow to the south of the Russian River near to Olivet Road, and the cute town of Sebastopol. The winery has a wonderful ethic and that is shown in the architecture, great gardens and staff. They have a wonderful team of people working there. While you can taste standing up at the beautiful bar, most tastings take place at the tables inside or outside on the spacious patios. They have extensive organic, ornamental and vegetable gardens surrounding the tasting room. Beyond those, you see the hillsides of vines. When you look outside from the tasting bar, you can see the canopy that covers the winery in the distance on the top of the hill. The wines stand out and they have become well known for their Pinot Noir! Quite a few of their wines are from their own estate vineyards, but they also source grapes from other parts of the Russian River Valley and Coastal Sonoma. The biggest district in Sonoma is the Coastal AVA, which extends along the Pacific shoreline. Map I

MacRostie Winery and Vineyards – Northern Russian River Valley – Wines: Rose, Chardonnay, Pinot Noir, Blends – 4605 Westside Road Healdsburg, CA 95448 – www.macrostiewinery.com – (707) 473-93038 – Hours: 11:00am–5:00pm Appointment – hospitality@macrostiewinery.com – This premium producer does their tasting in a lovely building perched on a hill in the Russian River Valley with wonderful views of the vines surrounding it. It is a seated tasting and they are very popular with a younger crowd so contact them well in advance. Map H

Manzanita Creek Winery – Healdsburg – Just Outside Downtown – Wines: Petite Syrah, Syrah, Zinfandel, Pinot Noir, Muscat – www.manzanitacreek.com – (707) 433-4052 They do no appear to be doing tastings currently.

Marimar Estate – Southern Russian River Valley – Graton Road – Wines: Chardonnay, Pinot Noir, Syrah–Tempranillo – 11400 Graton Rd. Sebastopol CA 95472 – www.marimarestate.com – (707) 823-43658 – Hours: 11:00am–5:00pm Appointment – This charming winery is owned by a Spanish family with a long winemaking history. It is off by itself on Graton road on the way to the charming little town of Occidental. The building is classic Spain and the tasting is elegant. The road from there to Occidental is winding and there are no other well-known wineries immediately nearby so it probably limits their traffic. But the location is lovely and the wines are well–made. Map I

Martin Ray Winery –Russian River Valley – Look for the Water Tower – Wines: Pinot Gris, Sauvignon Blanc, Chardonnay, Pinot Noir, Merlot, Cabernet Sauvignon, Gewürztraminer, Riesling – 2191 Laguna Rd. Santa Rosa CA 95401 – www.martinraywinery.com – (707) 823-2404 Hours: 11:00am–5:00pm Varies w/ Season – This is a cute winery that produces well–made, reasonably priced wines. The tasting is relaxed and may include a couple of their different labels. You can spot them as you approach because of their tall water tower looming over the road. The grounds are pretty and they have some nice picnic tables. The small tasting room has some interesting gifts and a nice, relaxed staff. If you are coming up from Guerneville Road, they are a bit farther than it looks like on the map. If you are reaching them from River Road going west, look for the Woodenhead Winery sign at the turn off. They are just down the road from the Joseph Swan Winery. Both Woodenhead and Joseph Swan make great stops. Map I

Martinelli Vineyards and Winery – Russian River Valley – Surprising Quality – Wines: Chardonnay, Pinot Noir, Syrah, Zinfandel, Gewürztraminer, Muscat Alexandria, Sauvignon Blanc – 3360 River Rd. Windsor CA 95965 – www.martinelliwinery.com – (707) 525-05708 – Hours: 10:00am–5:00pm – As you walk to this rustic building by the side of the road, you do not expect such a charming interior or such excellent wines. The family has been growing grapes alongside the Russian River and in Coastal Sonoma for many years. Their winery is located just a short distance off Highway 101 on River Road in a converted Hop Kiln building. It has fun, home style gifts and food items. They have a friendly and knowledgeable staff with picnic tables handy on the hillside and some deli items in a cooler. Map G

Martorana – Dry Creek Valley – Wines: Cabernet Sauvignon, Merlot, Zinfandel, Mozzafiato – 5956 W Dry Creek Rd, Healdsburg CA www.martoranafamilywinery.com – (707) 433-1909 – Hours: 11:00am–5:00pm – Appointment – info@martoranafamilywinery.com – A family run winery that has been farming vineyards in the area since the 1980's. Map J

Matanzas Creek Winery – Bennett Valley – Lavender and Wine – Wines: Merlot, Chardonnay, Sauvignon Blanc, Cabernet Sauvignon, Syrah, Rosé – 6097 Bennett Valley Rd.

Santa Rosa CA 95404 – www.matanzascreek.com – (800) 590-6464 – Hours: 10:00am–4:30pm Tours – This medium sized winery is located about 15 minutes west of Glen Ellen along a narrow road that is a bit of a winding ride, but well worth the trip. It is a beautiful, Asian style building with lavender gardens, pretty grounds, great views and gifts. Not surprisingly, they also offer estate made lavender products along with their seriously good wines. Take the time to stroll through the lavender gardens, with their lovely views of the Bennett Valley. Inside the tasting room beyond the tasting bar, look at the educational displays. From here, you can either return to the Sonoma Valley or continue on Bennett Valley Road to Santa Rosa, Highway 101 and the Russian River Valley wineries. Map D

Matrix Winery – Russian River Valley on the Edge of Dry Creek – Wines: Chardonnay, Pinot Noir, Zinfandel, Syrah, Cabernet Sauvignon – 3291 Westside Rd. Healdsburg CA 95448 – www.matrixwinery.com – (707) 433-1911 – Hours: 11:00am–5:00pm – This is a small winery tucked on the western hillsides at the northern edge between the Russian River and Dry Creek regions. They have a cute, intimate tasting room with nice views, and they are conveniently located. Their wines are nicely made from grapes from Alexander Valley, Russian River, Sonoma Coast and Dry Creek areas with an appeal to collectors. The winemaker pays a lot of attention to classic methods and the exact barrels for aging each varietal. Map H

Mauritson Family Winery – Dry Creek Valley – Rock Pile – Wines: Chardonnay, Zinfandel, Cabernet Sauvignon, Sauvignon Blanc, Syrah, Petite Syrah – 2859 Dry Creek Rd. Healdsburg CA 95448 – www.mauritsonwines.com – (707) 431-0804 Hours: 10:00am–5:00pm Appointment – This family has been growing grapes in this area since the 1860's when all of their wine was sent home to Sweden. Much of their original vineyards are now under water as part of Lake Sonoma, developed by the state in the 1960's. Today they have their vines on the dramatic ridges overlooking the lake in one of the county's newest AVA's called Rock Pile. This area is known for wonderful wines and it comes with a lot of effort. Some of the family vineyards are so steep and rough that everything has to be done by hand, no tractors. Fortunately, the tasting room is conveniently located at the intersection of Dry Creek Road and Lytton Springs Road, just two minutes from the Dry Creek General Store and ten minutes from downtown Healdsburg. They have a friendly, nicely decorated tasting room with tables and umbrellas outside. There are so few wineries that feature the wonderful grapes of Rockpile that it would be worth visiting here just for that reason. Hint: Visit earlier in the day since the western facing entranceway fills the tasting room with bright, afternoon sunlight and it can be a little overwhelming. Map J

Mayo Family Winery – Sonoma Valley – Wines: A Very Wide Variety – 13101 Arnold Dr. Glen Ellen CA 95442 – www.mayofamilywinery.com – (707) 938-9401 – Hours: 10:00am–6:30pm – They have two locations. This address in Glen Ellen is their main winery and tasting room offering their larger line of wines in a casual environment. It is located where Arnold Drive meets Highway 12. Their reserve room is located across from the Kenwood Winery. Although the name sounds Irish, the family is from France; the name was changed upon their arrival in the States. The winery tasting room is spacious where they feature well-made, reasonably priced wines. As a result, they tend to attract a younger crowd, which makes the place a lot of fun. Their reserve room in Kenwood is more intimate. Map D

Mayo Family Reserve – Sonoma Valley – Food Pairings – Wines: Chardonnay, Viognier, Zinfandel, Petite Syrah, Cabernet Sauvignon, Cabernet Franc, Zinfandel Port – 9200 Sonoma Highway Kenwood CA 95452 – www.mayofamilywinery.com – (707) 833-5504 – Hours: 10:00am–6:30pm – In their reserve room they do food pairings. They are next to VJB. It is a more expensive tasting than at the other, but fun. Calling it 'a 'food pairing' understates the experience. This is a pairing menu of seven courses, each with its own wine from their reserve list, created by their Executive Chef. It is a considerable amount of food and wine and not to be rushed. Map D

Mazzocco Vineyards – Dry Creek Valley near Alexander Valley – Wines: Chardonnay, Viognier, Carignane, Pinot Noir, Zinfandel, Cabernet Sauvignon, Merlot, Blends – 1400 Lytton Springs Rd. Healdsburg CA 95448 – www.mazzocco.com – (707) 431-8159 – Hours: 11:00am–5:00pm – This is a pretty winery perched up on a rise near the small local airport. The original winery owner lived in LA and liked the spot because he could fly up in his plane and walk next door. They make some great Chardonnay and Rhone-style wines. The tasting room is bright and airy with lovely views of the vineyards and a nice staff. It is currently owned by the Wilsons who have several wineries. It is a good stop between Dry Creek and Alexander valleys. Map J

Meadowcroft Wines – Sonoma Valley – At the Cornerstone Center Wines: Blanc de Blanc, French Colombard, Sauvignon Blanc, Chardonnay, Pinot Noir, Zinfandel, Syrah, Cabernet Sauvignon – 23574 Arnold Drive, Sonoma, CA 95476 – www.meadowcroftwines.com – (707) 934-4090 – Hours: 12:00pm to 4:00pm – Appointment. Map A

Meeker Vineyards – Downtown Healdsburg Tasting Room – Wines: Bordeaux, Cabernet Sauvignon, Merlot, Zinfandel, Petite Syrah, Syrah, Carignane, Ice wine – 5 Fitch St Unit B, Healdsburg, CA 95448 www.meekervineyards.com – (707) 431-2148 – Hours: 11:00am–4:00pm. Not shown on Map

Merriam Vineyards – On the Southern Edge of Healdsburg and Windsor – Wines: Bordeaux, Chardonnay – 11650 Los Amigos Road, Healdsburg, California 95448 – www.MerriamVineyards.com – (707) 433-4032 – Hours: 10:00am to 5:00pm. In the upper right hand corner of Map G

Merry Edwards – Russian River Valley – Well Respected– Wines: Pinot Noir, Sauvignon Blanc, Chardonnay – 2959 Gravenstein Highway North, Sebastopol, CA 95472 – www.merryedwards.com – (707) 823-7466 – Hours: 9:30–4:30 Appointment – This is a premier Pinot Noir maker. They do seated tasting and the wines are wonderful, the staff is friendly and knowledgeable and the place is appealing. The wines are not inexpensive. Their Sauvignon Blanc has received the highest scores ever awarded to an American Sauvignon Blanc, made from grapes grown in this valley where general wisdom says it could not be done. Map I

Michel-Schlumberger Wine Estate – Dry Creek Valley – Wines: Cabernet Sauvignon, Syrah, Pinot Noir, Merlot, Pinot Blanc, Chardonnay 4155 Wine Creek Rd. Healdsburg CA 95448 – www.michelschlumberger.com – (707) 433-7427 – Hours: 11:00am–5:00pm Appointment – This is a pretty winery in a classic building surrounding a courtyard, on a side road off of West Dry Creek Road. It has a European feel to the place, and the tasting areas make you feel like you're in a charming French home. They are by appointment. Our experience with them has always been pleasant. The only other winery on the same road is Mounts Family Winery, a small family place with a distinctly rustic tasting experience surrounded by vineyards. Map L

Mietz Cellars – Russian River Valley – Wines: Zinfandel, Sauvignon Blanc, Chardonnay, Merlot, Pinot Noir – 602 Limerick Lane Healdsburg, CA 95448 – www.mietzcellars.com – (707) 433-7103 – Hours: Appointment. Map G

Mill Creek Vineyards and Winery – The Edge of Dry Creek Valley by Russian River Valley – A Family Affair – Wines: Chardonnay, Syrah, Gewürztraminer, Sauvignon Blanc, Zinfandel – 1401 Westside Rd. Healdsburg CA 95448 – www.millcreekwinery.com – (707) 431-2121 Hours: 10:00am to 5:00pm – Seven members of the Kreck family make this place work from vineyard to bottle to shelf. They farm fifty plus acres of their own vines at the southern edge of the Dry Creek Valley, then make the wine and market it. They have a nice middle of the road price point that makes it easier to take some wine home with you. The tasting room is patterned on the Mills that were once common in the area, and the property includes a water wheel and mill pond. They have two large picnic areas and the tasting room is made mostly of local Redwood. Not surprisingly, their wine club is called the Sequoia Club. If you want to picnic with a larger group you should call them in advance. Map H

Mountain Terraces Winery and Vineyards – Sonoma Valley in the Hills – Wines: Cabernet Sauvignon – 3030 Cavedale Road Glen Ellen, CA 95442 – Not Currently Seeing visitors due to problems with the road – www.mountainterraces.com – (707) 996-1787 – info@mountainterraces.com. Map D

Mounts Family Winery – Dry Creek – Wines: Zinfandel, Petite Syrah, Cabernet Sauvignon, Cabernet Franc – 3901 Wine Creek Rd Healdsburg CA 95448 – www.mountswinery.com – (707) 292-8148 – Hours: Weekends and Appointment – The family has farmed these gorgeous hills on the west side of the Dry Creek Valley since the 1940's, and they are still a farming family, but now they are winemakers too. The winery is on site and the tasting room/barrel room is a low roofed workroom attached to a barn, but while the location is rustic, the views are great and the man who makes the wine pours it for you. The wines are well-made and the Petite Syrah stands out. When they are open to the public they put a sign up at the intersection of West Dry Creek Road and Wine Creek Road. Just past them on the same road is Michel-Schlumberger. Map L

Murphy-Goode Estate Vineyard and Winery –Downtown Healdsburg Tasting Room – Wines: Fumé Blanc, Chardonnay, Cabernet Sauvignon, Merlot, Pinot Noir, Zinfandel, Claret, Petit Verdot, Rosé, Muscat Canelli – 20 Matheson St. Healdsburg CA 95448 – www.murphygoodewinery.com –

(707) 431-7644 – Hours: 10:30–5:30 – Located just across the street from the Healdsburg Plaza. It is a spacious place with a nice tasting bar. The wines are well made. The vineyards and winery are in the central part of the Alexander Valley. Across the street from Hotel Healdsburg on Map F

Muscardini Cellars – Sonoma Valley – Tasting Room – Wines: Rosato di Sangiovese, Zinfandel, Barbera, Syrah, Cabernet Sauvignon – 8910 Sonoma Highway Kenwood CA 95452 – www.muscardinicellars.com – (707) 933-9305 – Hours: 11:00am–6:00pm – The wines are good examples of how much microclimates and grape selections can create unique and delicious results. The wines are well–made and full of that lovely Sonoma Valley depth and complexity. The tasting room is roomy with a large sitting porch out front and plenty of parking. Map D

Mutt Lynch Winery – Downtown Windsor – Wines: Chardonnay, Rose, Cabernet Sauvignon, Merlot – 9050 Windsor Road Windsor, CA 95492 – www.muttlynchwinery.com – (707) 687-5089 – Hours: 11:00am–6:00pm Appointment – Very Dog Friendly. Not shown on Map

Nalle Winery – Dry Creek Valley – Grass Covered Tasting Room – Wines: Zinfandel, Pinot Noir, Sauvignon Blanc, Chardonnay 2383 Dry Creek Rd. Healdsburg CA 95448 – www.nallewinery.com – (707) 433-1040 – Hours: 12–5 Saturday and other days by Appointment – This is a small winery that is covered with grass, and it is a lot more interesting looking on the outside than inside. They make interesting wines, but they are open on a rather irregular schedule. They have a small case production and sell out quickly. Map J

Nicholson Ranch – Southern Sonoma Valley on the edge of Los Carneros – Great Views – Wines: Chardonnay, Pinot, Syrah – 4200 Napa Rd. Sonoma CA 95476 – www.nicholson-ranch.com – (707) 938-8822 – Hours: 10:00am–6:00pm – They are located at the intersection of Napa Road (that takes you into downtown Sonoma) and Route 121. It sits on top of their caves and they have picnic tables alongside their pond. There are nice views from the grounds, although unfortunately you don't enjoy the views from the tasting room which is at the back of the building. It seems like they should be in the Los Carneros District rather than Sonoma Valley, but that area is just south of them, across the road. Being at that nexus of roads and districts must be rather confusing, because the wines they make have more in common with Los Carneros than the Sonoma Valley. They periodically do tours of their caves for groups. The property has livestock including Llamas and a Temple to Aphrodite. Map A

Notre Vue Estate and Balverne Winery – Chalk Hill – Wines: Pinot Noir, Sauvignon Blanc, Chardonnay – 11010 Estate Lane Windsor, CA 95492 – www.notrevueestate.com – Hours: 10:30am to 4:30pm by Appointment – (707) 433-4050. This is a stunning property that produce French inspired wines. Map G

Obsidian Winery - Sonoma Plaza - A wide variety of wines , Chard, Pinot Noir, Rose, Syrah, Malbec, Pitite Sirah, Petite Verdot, Cabernet Sauvignon Blends - 134 Church St, Sonoma, CA 95476 - obsidianwineco.com - (707) 255-4929 - Hours: 11-6 - After having their tasting room in the Cornerstone complex in the Los Carneros district south of the town, they have moved a new location on the Sonoma Plaza. It is a very appealing tasting room that you reach through a wide alley on the west side of the Plaza just behind the Sign of the Bear Cooking store. They very interesting, and properly priced wines. Map C

Old World Winery – Russian River Valley – Wines: Abundance, Luminous, Flow, Era, Bouschet – 850 River Road Fulton, CA 95439 www.oldworldwinery.com – (707) 490-6696 – Hours: 11:00am–5:00pm Appointment. A small winery on the south side of River Road not far from Highway 101. Map G

Optima Winery – Dry Creek Valley in the Timber Crest Center –Wines: Rose, Gewurztraminer, Zinfandel, Petite Syrah, Cabernet Sauvignon – 4791 Dry Creek Road Healdsburg, CA 95448 – www.optimawinery.com – (707) 431-8222 – Hours: 10:30am to 4:30pm – Appointment. Map J

Orsi Family Vineyards – Southside of Downtown Healdburg – Opened 2021 in Healdsburg – 2306 Magnolia Dr. Healdsburg CA 95448 – www.orsifamilyvineyards.com – (707) 732-4660 Hours: 10:30-4:30 – The Orsi family owns vineyards in various North Bay regions and this is the first time that they have their own tasting room. They are located across Highway 101 from downtown Healdsburg. They specialize in Italian wine grape varieties including biancolella, schioppettino and negroamaro along with better-known sangiovese, montepulciano and primitivo. They also make the classica California varietals. Map H

Pangloss Cellars – Downtown Sonoma Tasting – Wines: Rose, Sauvignon Blanc, Genache, Chardonnay, Pinot Noir, Zinfandel, Syrah, Cabernet Sauvignon – 35 E Napa St, Sonoma, CA 95476 – www.panglosscellars.com – (707) 933-8565 – They offer a private, focused, immersive seated tasting accompanied by a local cheese and charcuterie plate for each guest. Hours: 11:00am to 2:00pm – Appointment. Map C

Papapietro Perry – Dry Creek Valley in the Timber Crest Center – Popular Pinot – Wines: Pinot Noir, Zinfandel – 4791 Dry Creek Rd. Healdsburg CA 95448 – www.papapietroperry.com – (707) 433-0422 – Hours: 11:00am–4:00pm – They are known for their great wines, and it is a surprisingly small, low key tasting room considering the enthusiasm of their loyal clientele. But it is a fun tasting room. They are walking distance to Kokomo, Amphora and Peterson Wineries so you can stroll and taste. Map J

Paradise Ridge – Santa Rosa Hills with Views – 4545 Thomas Lake Harris Dr. Santa Rosa CA 95403 – www.prwinery.com – (707) 528-9463 – Hours: 11:00am–5:00pm – This winery sits at the crest of a hill overlooking Santa Rosa amid a sculpture garden. There are few other wineries in this area, although across Highway 101 there are some wineries in the nearby corporate park, and beyond that, the wineries on the southern edges of the Russian River. Map G

Passagio Wines – Sonoma Valley - Glen Ellen in the Jack London Center - 14301 Arnold Drive, Glen Ellen, CA 95442 - www.passaggiowines.com – Hours 11-5 Thurs-Sunday, Appointments on other days - (707) 719-9813 - They make wonderful wines and the Cindy Cosco, the winemaker often pours for you. Map E

Passalacqua Winery – Dry Creek Valley – Charming and Friendlyy – Wines: Sauvignon Blanc, Chardonnay, Zinfandel, Cabernet Sauvignon, Sangiovese, Primitivo – 3805 Lambert Bridge Rd. Healdsburg CA 95448 www.passalacquawinery.com – (707) 433-5550 – Hours: 11:00am–5:00pm – This is a small, family winery at the heart of the Dry Creek Valley in sight of the General Store. They make elegant wines poured in a well-lit, friendly tasting room with views of the valley. This is a family run winery, and the Passalacqua family has a long history here. Their own vineyards are farther south in the valley, and for the rest, they source their grapes from diverse areas, resulting in a interesting collection. The winery is just across from the tasting room, and being tight on space, the winemaking often spreads out into the walkway between the two buildings. They are located across the street from the Dry Creek Winery. Map J

Pasterick Wines – Dry Creek Valley – Cabernet Sauvignon, Syrah – 3491 W Dry Creek Rd, Healdsburg, CA 95448 – pasterickwine.com – (707) 433-4655 – Hours: Appointment - Small family winery, – Map J

Patz and Hall – South of the Sonoma Plaza – Wines: Chardonnay, Pinot Noir, Sparkling – 21200 8th St E, Sonoma, CA 95476 – www.patzhall.com (707) 265-7700 – Hours: Appointment – This is a premium Pinot producer that sources grapes from a number of regions. They do a lovely seated tasting, often on the back patio with views of the region. Map A

Paul Hobbs – Russian River Valley – Wines: Chardonnay, Cabernet Sauvignon, Cabernet Franc – 3355 Gravenstein Highway N, Sebastopol, CA 95472 – www.paulhobbswinery.com – (707) 824-9879 Hours: 10:00am to 2:00pm – Appointment – The owner is one of America's most significant consulting winemakers, and this is his home winery, where he offers his best. This is a fancy, seated tasting for the collector. Map I

Paul Mathew – Tasting Room – Russian River Valley – Wines: Grenache, Pinot Noir, Cabernet Franc, Gewurtraminer, Rose – 9060 Graton Road Graton, CA 95444 – (707) 861-9729 – Hours: 10:30am to 4:30pm – www.paulmathewvineyards.com. They are located in the little Graton downtown. Map I

Pech Merle Winery – Alexander Valley Downtown Geyserville Tasting Room – Wines: Rose de Syrah, Sauvignon Blanc, Viognier, Pinot Noir, Zinfandel, Carignan 21001 Geyserville Ave, Geyserville CA 95441 – www.pechmerlewinery.com – (707) 891-3015 – Hours: 11:00am–6:00pm – Appointment. Downtown Geyserville is on Map O

Pedroncelli Winery – Dry Creek Original – Wines: Sauvignon Blanc, Chardonnay, Sangiovese, Merlot, Zinfandel, Cabernet Sauvignon, Syrah, Petite Syrah, Port – 1220 Canyon Rd. Geyserville CA 95441 – www.pedroncelli.com – (800) 836-3894 – Hours: 10:00am–4:30pm – The vineyards have been in this family since 1927 and this is the oldest tasting room in the Dry Creek Valley. Of course, saying they are in the Valley does not describe their location because Canyon Road is one of the connections between the Dry Creek and Alexander

Valleys. They offer a wide variety of wines well suited to this area. During prohibition, they supplied home winemakers with grapes. While you could not sell wine, you could still make a limited amount for personal use and the Italian community was an especially good market for grape growers. The wines are from a mix of vines planted a hundred years ago and recently replanted vineyards. The tasting room is relaxed and pleasant. They feature the work of local artists. Map J

Pellegrini Family Vineyards – Southern Russian River Valley – Italian Family Tradition – Wines: Pinot Noir, Chardonnay, Cabernet Sauvignon, Merlot, Rosato, Carignane, Sauvignon Blanc, Zinfandel – 4055 W. Olivet Rd. Santa Rosa CA 95401 – ww.pellegrinisonoma.com – (707) 575-8465 – Hours: 10:30–4:30 – This big blocky, Italian style building towers over the surrounding vineyards and the tasting inside was at a small bar in the barrel room, but it may have changed. The design supports production over hospitality, but the wines are well-made. They are around the corner from the wineries of Olivet Road, including DeLoach and Hook and Ladder. Nearby are Lynmar and Ironhorse. Map I

Peterson Family Winery – Dry Creek Valley at the Timber Crest Center – Wines: Zinfandel, Cabernet Sauvignon, Petite Syrah, Sangiovese, Syrah, Muscat Blanc, Carignane Blend – 4791 Dry Creek Rd. Bldg. #7 Healdsburg CA 95448 – www.petersonwinery.com – (707) 431-7568 Hours: 11:00am–4:00pm – This is a pleasant, spacious tasting room with good wines just steps from Amphora and Kokomo. They have a pleasant staff and a pretty, well-lit tasting room. Map J

Pezzi King Vineyards – Downtown Healdsburg – Tasting Room – Wines: Chardonnay, Zinfandel, Merlot, Cabernet Sauvignon – 412 Hudson Street Healdsburg 95448 – www.pezziking.com – (707) 431-9388 – Hours: 10:00am–5:00pm – This winery has a long history in the Dry Creek Valley and currently has their offices and tasting room near the Front Street Wineries on Map F

Portalupi Wine – Downtown Healdsburg – Tasting Room – Wines: Graziano, Syrah, Primitivo, Pinot Noir, Vermintino, Arneis, Zinfandel, Petite Sirah, Charbono – 107 North St, Healdsburg, CA 95448 – www.portalupiwine.com – (707) 395-0960 – Hours:11:00am to 7:00pm – A downtown tasting room from long time growers in the area. Map F

Porter Creek Vineyards – Russian River Valley – River Edge Wines: Chardonnay, Viognier, Pinot Noir, Syrah, Carignane – 8735 Westside Rd. Healdsburg CA 95448 – www.portercreekvineyards.com – (707) 433-6321 – Hours: 11:00am–4:00pm – This is a small family run winery in a charming, traditional tasting room at the southern edge of Westside Road. They are nested amid Redwood trees and Oak trees just north of the Russian River. The wines are good and range from medium to moderately expensive. Their vineyards are Biodynamic and Organic. They are nearby the Gary Farrell Winery. Map H

Preston of Dry Creek – Organic Vineyards – Wines: Petite Syrah, Syrah, Sauvignon Blanc, Barbera, Mourvèdre, Cinsault, Carignane, Rousanne, Viognier, Vin Gris, Blends, Olive Oil, Olives – 9282 W. Dry Creek Rd. Healdsburg CA 95448 – www.prestonofdrycreek.com – (707) 433-3372 – Hours: 11:00am–4:00pm – This winery started off on a more conventional path with chemicals and larger production, and then Preston dramatically changed directions, reducing production and converting the vineyards to organic. You reach the winery via a gravel road at the top of the valley and the feeling of the place is authentic Dry Creek, with a welcoming garden complete with tables and shade. In true country style, the winery also has a bakery, olive oil samples and gracious grounds that make a relaxed, friendly experience. This is a great place to bring a picnic. Both their olive oil and their wines are good. They are around the corner from Ferrari Carano, nearby Zichichi and Bella wineries. Map L

Quivira Vineyards – Dry River Valley – High Tech Dry Creek – Wines: Zinfandel, Sauvignon Blanc, Syrah, Petite Syrah, Grenache, Rhone blends – 4900 W. Dry Creek Rd. Healdsburg CA 95448 – www.quivirawine.com – (707) 431-8333 – Hours: 11:00am–5:00pm – The wines for La Follete are also poured here. This is a Biodynamic/Organic winery with 'green' buildings. Surrounding the winery are vegetable gardens, chicken coops, pigs and goats. The roof is covered in solar panels. Between the gardens and the panels it looks like a science project gone wild, but they make good wines and do a fun tasting. Quivira was the name of a mythical Chinese city thought to be located on California's North Coast by the Spanish sailors who first explored the area. Why did they think that? Because they saw Chinese Junks sailing the coast when they first arrived! They were probably seeing stranded sailors from the great Chinese treasure fleets that sailed this coast in the early 1400's. After all, some of them were shipwrights so it's no surprise that they would build boats. The original owner collected maps of Quivira, and there was a gallery room displaying the maps. But when the winery was sold to the present owners the maps left, although the name remained. The hospitality tends to be variable; maybe the design of the building promotes a certain amount of eccentricity but it is a fun experience. Map L

Radio Coteau – Southern Russian River – Chardonnay, Pinot Noir, Syrah, Riesling, Zinfandel – 2040 Barlow Ln, Sebastopol, CA 95472 –radiocoteau.com – (707) 823-2578 – Hours – Grapes from both Sonoma and Mendocino's Anderson Valley Does not appear on Map.

Ram's Gate Winery – Los Carneros – Wines: Sauvignon Blanc, Chardonnay, Pinot Noir, Syrah, Cabernet Sauvignon – 28700 Arnold Dr, Sonoma, CA 95476 – www.ramsgatewinery.com – (707) 721-8700 – Hours: 11:00am–6:00pm – Appointment – This is an elegant winery that greets visitors as they arrive in Los Carneros from San Francisco. It has the feeling of a restaurant and bar with views. Map A

Ramazzotti Wines – Alexander Valley Tasting Room – Wines: Sparkling Rose, Frizzante Brut, Blanc de Blanc, Sauvignon Blanc, Pinot Grigio, Chardonnay, Zinfandel Rose, Barbera, Sangiovese, Cabernet Sauvignon – 21015 Geyserville Ave, Geyserville CA 95441 – www.ramazzottiwines.com – (707) 814-0016 – Hours: 11:00am–5:00pm. Map M

Raymond Burr Vineyards – Dry Creek Valley – An Actor's Vineyard – Wines: Cabernet Sauvignon, Cabernet Franc, Chardonnay – 8339 W. Dry Creek Rd. Healdsburg CA 95448 – www.raymondburrvineyards.com – (707) 433-8559 – Hours: 10:00am–5:00pm Appointment – This is a small, by appointment winery that was founded by the famous actor. They do tours of their orchids by appointment on Saturdays. It is informal and relaxed, at the upper edges of the valley. Map L

Red Car Wine – Russian River Valley Tasting Room – Wines: Chardonnay, Pinot Noir, Syrah – 8400 Graton Road Sebastopol, CA 95472 – www.redcarwine.com – (707) 829-8500 – Hours: 10:00am to 5:00pm – Appointment. Map I

Reeve Wines – Alexander Valley – Wines: Pinot Noir, Prism Riesling, Vermentino, Grenache, Chardonnay – 4551 Dry Creek Road Healdsburg, CA 95448 – www.reevewines.com – (707) 235-6345 – Hours: 11:00am–5:00pm – Appointment

– This is a charming family winery, tucked up on the eastern hills of the valley. The tasting is typically outside if weather permits and this area has great weather. Map A

Reprise Winery – Sonoma Valley Hills – Wines: A Variety –1700 Moon Mountain Road Sonoma, CA 95476 – www.repriswines.com (707) 931-7701 – Hours: 11:00am–5:00pm – Appointment – This sits on top of Moon Mountain to the north of the Sonoma Plaza. It is a narrow ride up there but you pass the famous Monte Rossa vineyards, known for its red soil. It is a beautiful location that sits in a bowl surrounded by the mountains. They do a tour of the hill top property in an ATV as part of the tasting and the wines tend to be on the lighter side with a couple of exceptions. Map D

Ridge Lytton Springs – Russian River Valley on the edge of the Alexander Valley – Big Zinfandels – Wines: Cabernet Sauvignon, Zinfandel, Grenache – 650 Lytton Springs Rd. Healdsburg CA 95448 – www.ridgewine.com – (707) 433-7721 – Hours: 11:00am–4:00pm – This is the northern branch of the well–respected Ridge Winery. Behind the stunning, modern building is acres of old vine Zinfandel, Petite Syrah, Alicante Bouschet and more. The tasting is fun and relaxed with views of the rolling hills filled with old vines. The wines deserve their great reputation. Ridge was one of the wines chosen to compete in the 1976 Judgment of Paris, although it did not win. But here is an interesting addition to the story. The movie Bottle Shock (2008) tells the story of the competition, and parts of it were filmed in downtown Sonoma. When the movie opened they staged a repeat of the competition including the original wineries. This time Ridge won! They have some of the largest organic vineyards in Sonoma. Lytton Springs Road connects the Dry Creek Valley to the Alexander Valley, so this makes a great tasting stop as you travel from one valley to the other. Map J

Robert Young Estate Winery – Alexander – Famous Chardonnay from Alexander Valley – Wines: Chardonnay, Merlot, Cabernet Sauvignon, Cabernet Franc, Blends – 4960 Red Winery Rd. Geyserville CA 95441 – www.ryew.com – (707) 431-4811 – Hours: 10:00am–4:30pm– This is a wonderful winery with a hilltop tasting room that overlooks the valley. It sits on the eastern side of Alexander Valley. Most of their grapes are sold to other premium producers, most notably Chateau St. Jean, but what they make for themselves is good. It is a charming experience in a great location. Map M

Robledo Family Winery – Southwest Sonoma Valley on the edge of Los Carneros – Down Home Friendly – Wines: Chardonnay, Pinot Grigio, Moscato, Cabernet Sauvignon, Merlot, Pinot Noir, Pinot Blanc, Sauvignon Blanc. 21901 Bonness Rd. Sonoma CA 95476 – www.robledofamilywinery.com – (707) 939-6903 – Hours: 10:00am–5:00pm, Sunday until 4:00pm by Appointment. The Robledo family is a large clan and they make great wines. The tasting room is down–home friendly and always worth a visit. During the Passport weekends, when wineries are open to anyone who has purchased a pass and a glass, this is the one of our favorite places to visit. The wines are good and a real value. The Robledo family and their story is an important part of the fabric that makes Sonoma special. The tasting/barrel room is comfortable and spacious with large tables and a tasting bar where they display their many ribbons. They are nearby to Roche Family, the next listing. Map D

Roche Winery and Vineyards – Sonoma Valley – At the Plaza and the Estate – Wines: Chardonnay, Pinot Noir, Merlot, Syrah, Cabernet Sauvignon, Muscat Cannelli, Tamarix blend of Chardonnay, Syrah and Pinot Noir – At the Plaza – 122 West Spain St. Sonoma CA 95476 – At the Winery – 22097A Bonness Rd, Sonoma, CA – 95476 www.rochewinery.com – (800) 825-9475 – Hours: Check the website for the two locations – This long time Los Carneros grower has a lovely winery in the southeast corner of the Sonoma Valley just north of the Los Carneros line. They also have a tasting room at the northeast corner of the Sonoma plaza in a charming little craftsman style bungalow. They make wonderful, properly priced wines and they have a friendly staff. In the nicer weather, which is the norm here, they have an outdoor tastings. The Plaza tasting room is next door to 'the Girl and the Fig' restaurant. Map A & C

Rodney Strong Vineyards – Russian River Valley – A Unique Building – Wines: Sauvignon Blanc, Chardonnay, Pinot Noir, Merlot, Syrah, Cabernet Sauvignon, Meritage, Zinfandel, Port – 11455 Old Redwood Highway. Healdsburg CA 95448 – www.rodneystrong.com – (707) 433-6511 – Hours: 10:00am–5:00pm – This is a unique wooden building with a cool self-tour where you walk around the perimeter and look down on the various tanks. There is a great story that goes along with the winery, and that is what you will see depicted on the walls as part of the tour. This is a relatively large winery for this area. Rodney Strong was a song and dance man who, together with his wife, started in the wine business in a funny way. They would come up to this area, buy wine, take it back to their home, and blend it. They lived by a yacht club and they would sell the wine from their home. Rodney decided that he could not be an old song and dance man, but he could be an old winemaker, so they bought their first vineyard in Sonoma and the rest is history. Today the winery is owned by another family, but the reputation of Rodney Strong continues. They make good, solid wines poured in a interesting tasting room suspended above the winery. They have a nice gift section and are located on the same driveway as the J Winery, and the location is convenient to both Highway 101 and Healdsburg. Map H

Roth Estate Winery – Russian River Valley Chalk Hill – Wines: Cabernet Sauvignon, Syrah, Pinot Noir, Chardonnay, Merlot – 10309 Chalk Hill Road Healdsburg, CA 95448 – ww.www.rothwinery.com – (707) 836-7030 – Hours: 11:00am–5:00pm – Appointment – concierge@rothwinery.com – This sits across the road from the Chalk Hill Winery and it is owned by the same people. It is a fun, popular place, although the drive to both places requires a great number of turns. Map G

Rued Winery – Dry Creek Valley – Six Generations – Wines: Chardonnay, Sauvignon Blanc, Zinfandel, Cabernet Sauvignon – 3850 Dry Creek Road Healdsburg, CA 95448 – www.ruedvineyards.com – (707) 433-3261 – Hours: 11:00am–4:00pm This family has been farming in Sonoma for 125 years and six generations, but this is actually a new tasting room, conveniently located just up the road from the Dry Creek Store. It is charming, the staff is knowledgeable and Northern Sonoma friendly and the wines are good. Being a newer winery, the price point is good, and the views of the valley are lovely. It is nearby Truett Hurst and the Timber Crest Center and Unti. Map J

Russian Hill Estate Winery – Russian River Valley – Great Views in Russian River Valley – Wines: Pinot Noir, Syrah, Chardonnay, Port – 4525 Slusser Rd. Windsor CA 95452 – www.russianhillestate.com – (707) 575-9428 – Hours: 10:00am–4:00pm Thursday to Monday – This pretty winery sits behind the Santa Rosa Airport. When you are in the tasting room, or enjoying the patio out back, the views of the rolling hills are great. They are just north of the well-known Sonoma Cutrer Winery, and you can see the restored Hop Kiln building which is part of Sonoma Cutrer's operations. They have nice wines, a good, relaxed staff and a nice tasting experience off the beaten path. Map G

Saini Vineyards – Dry Creek Valley – Sauv Blanc, Chenin Blanc, Grenache, Rosso, Zinfandel, Carignane – 507 Dry Creek Rd, Healdsburg, CA 95448 – sainivineyards.com – (707) 433-8477 – Hours: 12-4 Thurs-Sunday Appointment - Small family winery, since 1917, - Map J

Saint Anne's Crossing – Sonoma Valley – Wines: Zinfandel, Cabernet Sauvignon, Malbec, Petite Verdot – 8450 Sonoma Highway, Kenwood, CA 95452 – www.stannescrossing.com – (707) 598-5200 – Hours: 11:00am–5:00pm – It was started by the Wilsons to feature Dry Creek Zinfandel, but over the years it has stretched out a bit. This is a pretty tasting room, that sits in front of the winery. It has a nice patio out back. It is across the street from Chateau St. Jean. Map D

Saint Francis Vineyard and Winery – The Top of the Sonoma Valley – Wines: Chardonnay, Cabernet Sauvignon, Merlot, Zinfandel, Syrah – 100 Pythian Rd. Santa Rosa CA 95409 – www.stfranciswine.com – (888) 675-9463 – Hours: 10:00am–5:00pm – The tasting room is a dramatic Spanish style visitor's center that was designed to take advantage of the wonderful views of their vineyards and the mountains in the distance. You can see the separate winery building tucked against the mountains at the back of the property. The traffic light at the intersection of Highway 12 and Pythian Road makes it a great 'northern limit' for a Sonoma Valley tour on a busy day. Whenever you can make it easy and safe to turn around, you should take advantage of that. The tasting room is spacious, with a long tasting bar and a nice gift area. The staff is pleasant and there are lovely patios and grounds, including covered areas to sit and chat. They also do wonderful seated food pairings by appointment. Map D

Sangiacomo Wines – Sonoma Valley – A long time Los Carneros Grower – Pinot Noir, Chardonnay – 21545 Broadway, Sonoma CA 21545 – sangiacomowines.com – (707) 934-8445 – Hours: Appointment – The tasting is at their ranch just off Broadway south of the Sonoma Plaza. The family has been growing grapes for local wineries for many years, and finally they decided to use some of the grapes for their own label. Map B

Sbragia Family Vineyards – Dry Creek Valley – Great Views - Wines: Sauvignon Blanc, Chardonnay, Merlot, Zinfandel, Cabernet Sauvignon – 9990 Dry Creek Rd Geyserville CA 95441 – www.sbragia.com – (707) 473-2992 – Hours: 11:00am–5:00pm – This dramatic winery is perched on a hillside at the north end of the Dry Creek Valley across from the dam that formed Lake Sonoma and it has the best views of any winery in the valley. On the maps, this looks farther than it is, but it is just five minutes north of the popular Ferrari–Carano winery. It is worth a visit, being family owned and run, the hospitality is good. Ed Sbragia was the head winemaker at Beringer for many years and his sure hand is evident in this wonderful collection of wines. They do tastings both inside at the bar and sitting outside on the spacious patio. They offer reserve tastings for the enthusiast on the weekend, in a small, charming building called the Ark. Map L

Scherrer Winery – Southern Russian River – Chardonnay, Pinot Noir, Syrah, Zinfandel, Cabernet Sauvignon, Grenache, Rose' – 4940 Ross Rd, Sebastopol, CA 95472 – scherrerwinery.com – (707) 823-8980 – Hours: Limited Appointments at the Estate. Also available at the Barlow – Small – Map I

Scribe Winery – Southern Sonoma Valley on the edge of Los Carneros – Wines: Rose, Chardonnay, Pinot Noir, Syrah, Cabernet Sauvignon – 2100 Denmark St, Sonoma, CA 95476 – (707) 939-1858 – Hours: 11:30am to 4:00pm – Appointment – They are located on the hillsides south of the Sonoma Plaza, just north of the Los Carneros line. They have two sites for tasting, a casual hillside with blankets to sit on the grass for the wine club members, and a restored white house that they use for general tasting that can be seen from Napa Road. It is very popular with a younger crowd. Map A

Schug Carneros Estate Winery – Los Carneros – Views and Pinot – Wines: Sauvignon Blanc, Chardonnay, Pinot Noir, Merlot, Cabernet Franc, Cabernet Sauvignon, Syrah, Blanc de Noirs Sparkling Pinot Noir – 602 Bonneau Rd. Sonoma CA 95476 – www.schugwinery.com – (707) 939-9363 – Hours: 10:00am–5:00pm – They are a Carneros Estate Winery, wonderfully convenient to San Francisco. Many of their grapes grow on the gorgeous hillsides right outside the charming tasting room door. They have a knowledgeable staff, with excellent wines and a great, German-style building. Schug was the founding winemaker at the revered Joseph Phelps Winery in Napa, and was involved in the production of Napa's first Bordeaux blend. However, his love of Burgundy wines, Pinot Noir and Chardonnay, led him to open his own winery in this pretty canyon. The wines are well–made and a good deal. They do tours by appointment. They have great views of Carneros, and the Bay and they are just minutes from Gloria Ferrer, Jacuzzi, Cline & Roche. Map B

Sebastiani Vineyards and Winery – Downtown Sonoma – A Long Tradition – Wines: Cabernet Sauvignon, Merlot, Barbera, Zinfandel, Pinot Noir – 389 – 4th St. E. Sonoma CA 95476 – www.sebastiani.com – (707) 938-5532 – Hours: 10:00am–5:00pm – This old time Sonoma winery is near the Sonoma Plaza. In the 1990's, they sold their bulk wine division and began concentrating on premium wines, producing high–quality, reasonably–priced wines. Take the time to visit the historic barrel room that use for events inside the beautiful visitor center. The Sebastiani Winery opened for business in 1906. They were able to operate through prohibition because Samuele got a permit to make sacramental wine for the churches. Even though they were closely monitored by the government, they didn't know that he had buried tanks and special valves in the winery. After making the approved volume of wine, when the revenue official left, he would sent the wine into these hidden tanks and make more. By the time Prohibition finished he had hundreds of thousands of gallons of wine aging in the cool tanks underground. The family sold the winery in 2009, however members of the family continue in the wine business, and own vineyards and wineries in the area. Map C

Seghesio Winery – Healdsburg – Traditional Healdsburg – Wines: Zinfandel, Arneis, Pinot Grigio, Barbera, Sangiovese, Italian varietals – 14730 Grove St. Healdsburg CA 95448 – www.seghesio.com – (707) 433-3579 – Hours: 10:00am–5:00pm – The winery is located five minutes from the plaza in downtown Healdsburg; the town simply grew up around them. They planted their first vineyards in 1895, and they continue to make good solid wines. The winery has bocce courts, a nice gift section, gracious grounds, and a stunning tasting room that looks through a glass wall at the barrels aging in their cellar. The tasting bar is nice and long. They produce widely respected Italian varietals, and they offer food pairings and library wines. They do great special events that are a lot of fun. One of the big benefits is their location, being just minutes from the Healdsburg plaza, you can include them in a tour of the downtown tasting rooms, or stop there on the way from one valley to another. The original family sold the winery but the new owners have happily changed very little. Map F

Selby Winery –Downtown Healdsburg – Tasting Room – Wines: Chardonnay, Sauvignon Blanc, Rosé, Syrah, Pinot Noir, Old Vine Zinfandel, Port, Merlot, Petite Syrah, Dolcetto, Semillon, Dessert – 215 Center St. Healdsburg CA 95448 – www.selbywinery.com – (707) 431-1288 – Hours: 11:00am

–5:30pm – This is a small tasting room conveniently located across from the Oakville market and near the Healdsburg Plaza. Susie Selby is the winemaker and she sources her grapes from various areas around northern Sonoma. The tasting room is intimate, pretty and friendly and the wines are well made. Map F

Siduri Wines – Downtown Healdsburg – Wines: Pinot Noir – 235 Healdsburg Ave, Healdsburg, CA 95448 – www.siduri.com – (707) 578-3882 – Hours: 10:00am–4:30pm Friday – Sunday Appointment – The tasting room is in downtown Healdburg by the H2 Hotel. The wines are well regarded. Map F

Silver Oak Cellars – Alexander Valley – Big Reds – Wines: Cabernet Sauvignon Blend – 7300 Hwy 128 Healdsburg CA 95448 – www.silveroak.com – (707) 942-7082 – Hours: 9:00am–4:00pm – They produce an appealing Cabernet Sauvignon blend that they pour at both of their wineries; the other is in the Oakville section of the Napa Valley. There are distinct differences between the two areas; the Alexander Valley grapes produce softer and less tannic wines, the Napa wines are bigger and meaner. Just kidding! This is a state of the art winery and a gracious hospitality building on the Mayacamas benchlands. Map M

Simi Winery – Healdsburg – Great Tradition now in Corporate Ownership – Wines: Sauvignon Blanc, Chardonnay, Merlot, Cabernet Sauvignon – 16725 Healdsburg Ave. Healdsburg CA 95448 – www.simiwinery.com – (707) 433-6981 – Hours: 10:00am–5:00pm – Tours – This winery was founded in 1876 in San Francisco by two Italian brothers. In 1881, they moved the winery to Healdsburg. The daughter of one of the founders, Isabelle, ran the winery for many years and continued to make wine right through Prohibition, storing it in the cellars. While she had to sell many of their vineyards to survive, when Prohibition ended, she was one of the few companies with wine ready to sell. She sold the winery in 1970 and it has changed hands several times since then. They still make great wines; they have a friendly staff, and have both a gift and a picnic area. They are located just a few minutes from the Healdsburg Plaza. Map F

Simoncini Vineyards – Dry Creek Valley – Wines: Zinfandel Rose, Sauvignon Blanc – 2303 W. Dry Creek Road Healdsburg, CA 95448 – www.simoncinivineyards.com – (707) 433-8811 – Hours: Seatings at 11:00am–2:00pm – Appointment – This is a charming family run winery on a stretch of the road with very few wineries, even though, as the crow flies, it is quite nearby. Their caves are cool and Dry Creek Valley is one of the prettiest areas in Northern California. Map J

Skip Stone Ranch – Collectors Alexander Valley – Wines: Oliver's Blend, Faultline Vineyard, Viognier, Rose, Malbec, Merlot 2505 Geysers Road Geyserville CA 95441 – (707) 433-9124 – Hours: Appointment – info@skipstoneranch.com – This is a tasting in the garden behind the home of the wealthy owner. The consulting winemaker is Phillipe Melka, who is known for making so many expensive Napa Cabs. From the seating area the views of the vineyards are great, although this area was hard hit in the 2019 fire that started a short distance away. Map O

Small Vines – Region – Pinot Noir – 1600 Barlow Ln, Sebastopol, CA 95472– website – (707) 823-0886– Hours: 10-4:30 closed Sundays by Appointment Expensive– Organic winery, high end producer – Map G

Soda Rock Winery – Southern Alexander Valley – Chardonnay, Sauvignon Blanc, Merlot, Primitivo, Zinfandel, Cabernet Franc, Cabernet Sauvignon, Malbec – 8015 Highway 128 Healdsburg, CA 95448 – www.sodarockwinery.com – (707) 433-3303 – Hours: 11:00am–5:00pm – This is owned by the Wilson family. The location has a long wine making tradition. The 2019 Alexander Valley fire destroyed the buildings on this site but they are back in business. Map N

Sojourn Cellars – Downtown Sonoma – Tasting Room Changes Ahead – Wines: Cabernet Sauvignon, Pinot Noir – As of the beginning of 2021 they are located at 141 East Napa St. Sonoma CA 95476 – But, they are projected to move to their new winery location at 18701 Gehricke Rd. Sonoma CA – www.sojourncellars.com – (707) 933-9753 – Hours: 10:00am–5:00pm Appointment – They started with Pinot Noir and Cabernet Sauvignon. Why two wines? Because the two friends who started the winery like those two wines, so that is what they made. Later they added a Chardonnay. It is by appointment, for a seated tasting at a lovely conference table in the front room. The wines are elegant as is the experience. The current tasting room is just a short walk off the Plaza, down the street that was used for the the movie Bottle Shock, about the Judgment of Paris. It beautifully portrayed a Parisian street with the help of a green screen. Map C

Sonoma Cutrer – Russian River Valley – Big Label with Croquet – Wines: Chardonnay, Pinot Noir – 4401 Slusser Rd

Windsor CA – www.sonoma-cutrer.com – (707) 528-1181 – Hours: 10:00am–4:00pm This is a well-known label that is seen in many restaurants. It is a big estate and quite dramatic. The croquet courts were created by the original owner and are used for charity events. Map G

Spicy Vines Tasting Room – Downtown Healdsburg with Food Pairings – Wines: Pinot Noir, Chardonnay, Zinfandel, Cabernet Sauvignon – 441 Healdsburg Ave Healdsburg, CA 95448 – www.spicyvines.com – (707) 927-1065 – Hours: Check Website for Appointments. Map F

Square Peg Winery – Russian River Valley – Dry Farmed Premium Pinot Noir by Allocation Outside Occidental – 4728 Stoetz Lane Sebastopol CA 95472 – www.squarepegwinery.com – (707) 827-1711 – Hours: 11:30am to 4:30pm. Not shown on Map I

Starlite – Alexander Valley – Wines: Cabernet Sauvignon, Viognier, Zinfandel – 5511 Highway 128, Geyserville CA 95441 – www.starlitevineyards.com – (650) 464-7154 – Hours: 11:00am–5:00pm – Appointment – They sit alongside Highway 128 just north of Alexander Valley Road. They are nearby Jordan, Foley of Sonoma, Robert Young and Reeves. Map M

Stephen and Walker – Downtown Healdsburg – Tasting Room – Wines: Cabernet Sauvignon, Pinot Noir, Port, Zinfandel – 243 Healdsburg Ave. Healdsburg CA 95448 – www.trustwine.com – (707) 431-8749 – Hours: 11:00am–7:00pm – Their other name is the Trust Winery Limited. This is a simple tasting room just a few steps off the Plaza that sells the products of a wine making couple, hence, the two names. It is a long tasting bar, in a brightly lit room, with a collection of ceramics displayed for sale. The families that run it have been growing grapes and making wines in the area for years. Map F

Stonestreet Winery – Alexander Valley Grand Estate – Wines: Merlot, Cabernet Sauvignon, Chardonnay, Sauvignon Blanc – 7111 Highway 128 Healdsburg CA 95448 – www.stonestreetwinery.com – (707) 473-3333 – Hours: 10:00am–5:00pm varies with season – This winery sits about midway up the Alexander Valley, with the entrance just south of where Highway 128 turns and becomes Alexander Valley Road on the way to Healdsburg. It is a beautiful estate winery using hillside grapes. The views are pretty spectacular and from the winery, you can see the vineyards across the valley. This is a Jackson Family winery (of Kendall Jackson fame). They are across the way from Silver Oak Winery, and nearby are Robert Young and Foley of Sonoma. Map M

Stone Edge Farms – Sonoma Valley – Two Locations – Wines: Bordeaux Blends – 5700 Cavedale Rd, Glen Ellen, CA 95442 – (707) 935-6520 – Appointment – concierge@stoneedgefarm.com – The original location is at the south west edge of the Sonoma Valley, tucked up against the hills. The above location is at the upper edge of the Mayacamas Mountains along the Napa border on Cavedale Road. These are ultra-premium wines and both properties are sustainable. Map D

Stuhlmuller Vineyard – Alexander Valley – Wines: Cabernet Sauvignon, Zinfandel, Chardonnay – 4951 West Soda Rock Lane, Healdsburg, CA 95448 – www.stuhlmullervineyards.com - (707) 431-7745 Hours: Appointment Friday through Monday – This vineyard and winery sits on the western banks of the Russian River way down the road in Alexander Valley. It has great views of the valley and the wines are excellent. You can picnic on the patio. Map M

Suncé Winery – Russian River Valley – Wines: Chardonnay, Sauvignon Blanc, Pinot Noir, Zinfandel, Cabernet Sauvignon, Meritage, Barbera, Sangiovese, Cabernet Franc, Malbec, Syrah, Port, Petite Syrah – 1839 Olivet Rd. Santa Rosa CA 95401 – www.suncewinery.com – (707) 526-9463 – Hours: 10:30–5:00pm – Pronounced Soon–say! This is a cute tasting room. Considering how small and charming the place is, they produce an amazing variety of wines. They are one of the wonderful wineries on Olivet Road, including Hook and Ladder, DeLoach and Pellegrini. The staff is great, the tasting relaxed and they are convenient to numerous other wineries. Map I

Taft Street Winery – Russian River Valley – Sebastopol Casual – Wines: Merlot, Chardonnay, Pinot Noir, Sauvignon Blanc, Zinfandel, Syrah – 2030 Barlow Lane Sebastopol CA 95472 – www.taftstreetwinery.com – (707) 823-2049 – Hours: 11:00am–4:30pm Friday Sunday – This is a funny little winery that sits off a bit by itself outside of the charming town of Sebastopol. It looks more like a wood yard than a winery, except for those big tanks, and the barrel racks. But do not be deceived, they make good wines, the tasting room is quite cute, and the staff is wonderful. We especially love the innovative way they have used old barrels for tasting tables, topping them with clear glass and tucking their numerous ribbons and medallions into the hollow below. They are around the corner from the restaurant, Underwood Bar and Bistro in Graton. Map I

Talisman Wines – Glen Ellen Tasting Room – Wines: Pinot Noir – 13651 Arnold Dr, Glen Ellen, CA 95442 – www.talismanwine.com – (707) 721-1628 – Hours: 11-5 Appointment. This charming tasting room sits in the little downtown Glen Ellen. The vineyards are in the southeast part of the valley where it is cool enough to grow good Pinot Noir. Located in the Glen Ellen downtown which is Map E

Talty Winery – Dry Creek Valley – Wines: Petite Syrah, Zinfandel – 7127 Dry Creek Road Healdsburg, CA 95448 – www.taltyvineyards.com – (707) 433-8438 – Hours: 12:00pm to 4:00pm – Appointment – Very much a small family grower and wine maker. Map L

Tara Bella Winery – Russian River Valley – Wines: Cabernet Sauvignon – 3701 Viking Road Santa Rosa, CA 95401 – www.tarabellawinery.com – (707) 544-9049 – Hours: Appointment – tarabellavines@gmail.com – This is a little jewel of a winery that quite surprisingly produces Cabernet, a heat loving grape, in the cool Russian River from their six acres of vines. Map I

The Spire Collection – Alexander Valley – Chardonnay, Sauvignon Blanc, Merlot, Primitivo, Zinfandel, Cabernet Franc, Cabernet Sauvignon, Malbec – 10075 Highway 128 Healdsburg, CA 95448 – www.membershipbyspire.com – (800) 544-7273 – Hours: 10:00am–3:30pm. On the site of the Fieldstone winery. Map N

Thomas George Estate – Russian River Valley – Hillside Caves – Wines: Chardonnay, Pinot Noir, Zinfandel, Viognier – 8075 Westside Road, Healdsburg CA 95448 – www.thomasgeorgeestates.com – (707) 431-8031 – Hours: 11:00am–5:00pm – They are located at the old Davis Bynum site that they have beautifully redone. They often taste in the cave. It sits on the hills above the Russian River and is reached by a steep driveway, leading up to a pretty clearing with picnic areas next to the tasting room. The vineyards in this area have always produced exceptional wines, so they are building on good foundations. This is an appealing and enjoyable experience. Map H

Three Sticks Wines – Downtown Sonoma Tasting Room – Wines: Pinot Blanc, Castenada Rose, Chardonnay – 143 W. Spain St, Sonoma, CA 95476 – www.threestickswines.com – (707) 996-3328 – Hours: 9:00am to 5:00pm – Appointment – The tasting of these premium wines takes place in a beautifully restored historic Adobe steps from the Sonoma Plaza. Map C

Thumbprint Cellars – Downtown Healdsburg Tasting Room – Wines: Bordeaux, Burgundy, Rhone, Zinfandel – 102 Matheson Street Healdsburg CA 95448 – www.thumbprintcellars.com – (707) 433-2393 – Hours: 11:00am–6:00pm – This is a fun tasting room facing the Healdsburg plaza. They make good, moderately priced wines, and they have a fun staff. They have a wonderful, easy going style. Map F

Tin Barn Vineyards – Sonoma Valley – 8th Street Sonoma Winery Wines: Bordeaux, Burgundy, Rhone, Zinfandel – 21692 Eighth Street East, Suite 340 Sonoma, CA 95476 – www.TinBarnVineyards.com – (707) 938-5430 – Hours: 11:00am–4:00pm Saturday – Sunday – Weekdays Appointment – This is a small winery that produces good wines, located in a warehouse next to the Sonoma Airport. In that same complex are several small wineries, and some massive wine warehouses. Not surprisingly, the tasting is friendly and relaxed, it's hard to be overly formal when your front door is metal and the building is corrugated steel. The tasting room is high–ceilinged and spacious, and the interior windows look into the winery. Map A

Toad Hollow Vineyards – Downtown Healdsburg – Tasting Room – Wines: Bordeaux, Burgundy, Zinfandel – 409A Healdsburg Ave. CA 95448 – www.toadhollow.com – (707) 431-8997 – Hours: 10:00am–5:00pm – This is a cute tasting room just north of the Plaza with good wines and some neat gift items. They are a short walk to numerous other downtown tasting rooms and restaurants. The staff is fun and the tasting reasonable. Their vineyards are in the Russian River Valley. Map F

Trattore Farms Winery – Dry Creek Road – Wines: Burgundy, Bordeaux and Rhone plus Olive Oil & food pairings – 7878 Dry Creek Road Geyserville CA 95441 – www.trattorefarms.com – (707) 431-7200 – Hours: 11:00am–5:00pm Appointment. Grape vines and olive trees over forty rolling hillside acres. Trattore is Italian for tractor so obviously farming comes first here. Map L

Trentadue Winery –Alexander Valley – Italian Style – Wines: Sparkling, Zinfandel, Petite Syrah, Merlot, Cabernet Sauvignon, Viognier, Port, Old Patch Red. 19170 Geyserville Ave. Geyserville CA 95441 – www.trentadue.com – (707) 433-3104 – Hours: 10:00am–5:00pm This is an Italian American, family-owned and run winery with a long tradition that makes hospitality a way of life. They have created a beautiful property, well-made wines and a neat gift section. It feels like an Italian villa with gracious grounds and buildings suitable for events. Their original farm was in what is now Silicon Valley, and when the industry grew up around them, they moved to the Alexander Valley. Good choice! The name means 32 in Italian and the family comes originally from Bari on the Adriatic coast of Italy. They were part of thirty-two families that moved as a group. In 2019, the winery celebrated its 50th anniversary. Map O

Trione Vineyards – Alexander Valley – Hand Crafted – Wines: Bordeaux, Burgundy, Rhone Style Blend – 19550 Geyserville Avenue Geyserville, CA. 95441 – www.trionewinery.com – (707) 814-8100 – Hours: 10:00am–5:00pm Thursday – Sunday – This is a big winery just off of Highway 101, from a family with a long history in the Alexander Valley. It is located nearby Trentadue and the Frances Ford Coppola Winery. They make hand crafted wines from five estate vineyards in three Sonoma County appellations. Map O

Twomey Healdsburg – Russian River Valley – Great Building with Views – Wines: Pinot Noir – 3000 Westside Rd. Healdsburg CA 95448 – www.twomeycellars.com – (800) 505-4850 – Hours: 11:00am–5:00pm – When they bought this winery from Roshambo it was already known for its dynamic architecture, and its great views of the valley in the distance. Twomey, which is part of the Silver Oak family, wanted a good site to make Pinot Noir, and the Russian River Valley is ideal for those grapes. The other Twomey winery is in Northern Napa and is known for their Merlot blends. Like most of the Silver Oak wineries, the staff here is friendly and relaxed, the gift shop is rather classic in selection, and the wines are well made, without a lot of flash, but with depth and integrity. Map H

Ty Caton Vineyards – Sonoma Valley – Tasting Room – Wines: Syrah, Bordeaux – 8910 Sonoma Highway. Kenwood CA 95452 – www.tycaton.com – (707) 833-0526 – Hours: 11:00am–5:00pm - At Kenwood Village. Map D

Unti Vineyards – Dry Creek Valley – Respected Vineyard – Wines: Barbera, Syrah, Petite Syrah, Barbera Port – 4202 Dry Creek Rd. Healdsburg CA 95448 – www.untivineyards.com – (707) 433-5590 – Hours: 10:00am–4:00pm – This is a low keyed tasting in a newer space. The Unti Vineyard grapes are highly respected and sought after by winemakers, and their small winery produces wonderful wines. Map J

Valley of the Moon Location – Now Abbots Passage

Vérité – Alexander Valley Edge of Russian River Valley – 4611 Thomas Rd. Healdsburg CA 95448 – www.veritewines.com – (707) 431-3930 – Hours: 10:00am to 5:00pm Appointment – This is an ultra-premium winery owned by the Jackson Family, the owner of Kendall Jackson. They are located at the southern edge of the Alexander Valley nearby Lancaster, another ultra-premium producer. This area is where three American Viticulture Areas intersect, Alexander Valley, Knights Valley and Chalk Hill. Map N

Viansa Winery – Los Carneros on the Main Road – Italian Marketplace – Wines: Cabernet Sauvignon, Chardonnay, Barbera, Merlot, Nebbiolo Sangiovese, Dolcetto, Aleatico, Primitivo, Vernaccia, Pinot Grigio, Tocai, Cabernet Franc, Arneis, Rosato – 25200 Arnold Dr. Sonoma CA 95476 – www.viansa.com – (707) 935-5738 – Hours: 10:00am–5:00pm. As you travel north on Highway 121 to Sonoma from San Francisco, after you pass the Raceway, you will see the terracotta colored roof of Viansa on a hillside to the right. It was started by Vicki and Sam Sebastiani, Vicki and Sam equals Vi–an–sa, although it is no longer owned by the Sebastiani family. It was designed in the style of an Italian villa. And comes complete with terraced vines, olive trees, tiles and of course, Italian grapes varietals like Vernaccia and Pinot Grigio. Their Pinot Grigio vines were some of the first to be planted in Carneros. They have a Deli/Market and picnic tables with wonderful views of Los Carneros and the bird sanctuary in the distance. The only downside of this lovely winery is that, thanks to its location, it is a favorite spot for bus groups coming from San Francisco conventions. Map A

Viszlay Vineyards – Russian River Valley – Wines: Cabernet Sauvignon, Syrah, Pinot Noir, Zinfandel   851 Limerick Lane Healdsburg, CA 95448 – www.viszlayvineyards.com – (707) 481-1514 – Hours: 11:00am–5:00pm – Appointment. Map G

VJB Vineyards – Sonoma Valley – Tasting Room, Deli, Market and Espresso – Wines: Chardonnay, Cabernet Sauvignon, Syrah, Barbera, Super Tuscan – 9077 Sonoma Highway. Kenwood CA 95452 – www.vjbcellars.com – (707) 833-2300 – Hours: 10:00am–5:00pm – This may be the most welcoming winery in the Sonoma Valley because it contains not only a good tasting room with some stellar wines, but the Valley's best Italian deli and a beautiful Italian style courtyard filled with tables and a pizza kitchen. Of course, they also have an espresso bar and a wide range of interesting food items that they produce from their recipes. This is not surprising since the family is from Italy and they ran a successful restaurant in Santa Rosa for many years. Map D

Wellington Vineyards – Sonoma Valley – Owned by the Belmonte Family that owns VJB – Great Old Vines – Wines: A new collection – 11600 Dunbar Rd. Glen Ellen CA 95442 – www.wellingtonvineyards.com – (707) 939-0708 – Hours: 11:00am–5:00pm – This pretty tasting room offers some unwonderful wines. On the property are some beautiful old vines that go back to the prohibition era when growers shipped tons of grapes to home winemakers in the east. It is owned by the Belmonte family that also owns VJB. Map D

Westerhold Family Vineyards – Santa Rosa – Wines: Pinot Noir, Chardonnay – 4949 Grange Road Santa Rosa, CA 95404 – (707) 586-9391 – Hours: Appointment – info@westerholdwines.com. Not shown on Map

West Wines – Southern Dry Creek Valley – Wines: Cabernet Sauvignon, Sauvignon Blanc, Viognier, Blanc de Blanc 1000 Dry Creek Road Healdsburg, CA 95448 – (707) 433-2066 – Hours: 11:00am–5:00pm – Appointment. They are near the Wilson winery south of the Dry Creek Market. Map K

William Selyem – Russian River Valley – Wines: Zinfandel, Chardonnay, Pinot Noir, Gewurztraminer – 7227 Westside Road Healdsburg, CA 95448 – www.williamsselyem.com – (707) 433-6425 – tours@williamsselyem.com – This is a high-end producer in a remarkable building on Westside Road. They are very much by appointment and highly sought after. The grounds are interesting, with the buildings built around existing boulders. It is an unusual building for this region where most wineries tend towards ranch style or those that work in harmony with the land. This has a bit of an urban feel. Map D

Williamson Wines – Healdsburg Tasting Room with Pairings – Wines: Chardonnay, Pinot Noir, Merlot, Malbec, Shiraz, Cabernet Sauvignon – 134 Matheson Street Healdsburg CA 95448 – www.williamsonwines.com – (707) 473-0193 – Hours: 11:00am–7:00pm – These are some wonderful wines, and they take food pairing, designed to go with their wines, to a whole new level. They own and manage multiple vineyards, which may explain why they can offer such a wide variety of high-quality wines. Their home ranch is in the Dry Creek Valley, although the family is originally from Australia and they have that classic, relaxed hospitality. We have listed their first and current tasting room, located a few doors up Matheson Street from the Oakville Market, but they also have their Yoakim Bridge Estate, which can be visited by appointment. Map F

Williamson Yoakim Bridge Estate – Dry Creek Valley – A wide variety of high end wines – 7209 Dry Creek Rd. Healdsburg CA 95448 – www.williamsonwines.com – (707) 433-1500 – Hours: 11:00am– 5:00pm –Sunday Located in the upper part of the valley Williamson bought this property to feature their high end reserve wines and culinary experiences. This is expensive for Dry Creek, but very worth the price. They are near Ferrari–Carano, Sbragia, Zichichi, Preston and Bella. Map L

Wilson Winery – Dry Creek Valley Classic – Wines: Cabernet Sauvignon, Cabernet Franc, Zinfandel, Merlot, Syrah, Petite Syrah – 1960 Dry Creek Rd. Healdsburg CA 95448 – www.wilsonwinery.com – (707) 433-4355 – Hours: 11:00am–5:00pm – In terms of team spirit and winemaking skill, the Wilsons are stars. The outside of the building looks more like a barn than a winery, but do not be fooled, they produce some seriously good wines and pour them with style and enthusiasm. Folks leaves Wilson with a smile, and often a case or two of wine, as a result of good management, great teamwork and fun. The tasting room includes some nice gift items, wonderful views of the vineyards, and tables outside on the patio. The winery is one of the first places you come to on the left side as you travel up the valley from Healdsburg. The parking lot is just past the building. Look for the huge sculpture of a wolf in their front yard. Map F

Woodenhead Winery – Russian River Valley– Wines: Pinot Noir, Zinfandel – 5700 River Road, Santa Rosa 95401 – www.woodenheadwine.com – (707) 887-2703 – Hours: 10:30 to 4:30 Thursday – Monday – The entrance to this winery is just off River Road on the right as you head west. You reach the tasting room via a steep driveway, and then a series of stairs. The tasting room is intimate and friendly. The wines are good, the staff is knowledgeable and the owners may pour for you. They have some interesting items in their gift area, and the overall feeling in the tasting room is fun and social. They are near Martin Ray and Joseph Swan. Map G

Wren Hop – Region – Pinot Noir – 3701 Mark West Station Rd, Windsor, CA 95492 – wrenhop.com – (707) 836-1715 – Hours: 10-4 Appointment – Very small high-end producer, Very Cool website – Map I

Zialena Winery – Alexander Valley – Wines: Cabernet Sauvignon, Zinfandel – 21112 River Road Geyserville CA 95441 – www.zialena.com – (707) 955-5992 – Hours: 10:00am – 4:30pm Appointment – Info@zialena.com – A family winery that has its history here for four generation, back to when the first member came from Carrara Italy to work in the Italian Swiss Colony winery. They have built a very modern winery and tasting room on their land in the northeast part of the valley nearby downtown Geyserville. Map O

Zichichi Vineyard and Winery – Dry Creek Valley – Wines: Zinfandel, Petite Syrah – 8626 W. Dry Creek Rd. Healdsburg CA 95448 – www.zichichifamilyvineyard.com – (707) 433-4410 – Hours: 11:00am–4:00pm – This is a small winery from a family that came here from New Orleans. They have a pretty tasting room with nice views of the northern valley. They often do both bar and barrel tastings. This is a nice treat since the barrel tasting lets people see how the wines develop during their process. Navigation: They are located at the corner of West Dry Creek Road and Yoakim Bridge Road. Map L

Zina Hyde Cunningham Winery – Tasting Room on the Sonoma Plaza inside the Ledson Hotel– Wines: Sauvignon Blanc, Chardonnay, Pinot Noir, Carignane, Zinfandel – www.zinawinery.com – (707) 895-9462 – The roots of this winery go back to the mid-1800's in Sonoma and Mendocino and it is associated with the Ledson Winery. Map C

ZO Wines – Dry Creek Valley– Wines: Zinfandel, Sauvignon Blanc, Chardonnay, Viognier, Pinot Noir – 3232 Dry Creek Road Healdsburg CA 95448 – www.zowines.com – (707) 794-6060 – Hours: 11:00am–5:00pm – Appointment – info@zowines.com – A small family winery at the south end of Dry Creek Road just north of Healdsburg. Map K

Zouzounis Wines (Previously Deux Amis) – Windsor Corporate Park – Pinot Noir, Cabernet Sauvignon, Petite Syrah and a Port, Zinfandels – 7680 Bell Road, Windsor (Windsor Beverage District) – www.zouzouniswines.com – (707) 431-7945 – Hours: 1:00pm – 5:00pm Saturday to Sunday Appointment. Not shown on Map

Notes

Other Titles by These Authors

AmicisTours.com

A Tour Guide's Napa Valley
A Tour Guide's Sonoma Wine Country
Sonoma Navigator, Maps & Highlights
Napa Navigator, Maps & Highlights
Wine Country in Shorts, A Tour Guide's Stories

Catch Our TV Show 'Wine Countery in Shorts'

PlanetaryCalendar.com
Published Annually since 1949

Planetary Calendar Astrology Forecasts & Health Hints
Two Wall Sizes, a Pocket Size, a Day Planner &
a Digital Version for your Phone and Computer
The Companion Book
'Planetary Calendar Astrology,
Moving Beyond Observation to Action'

*Watch the Author's Monthly Forecasts
at Planetary Calendar.com*

SpaceAndTime.com

From the 'Tango' Series
Feng Shui and the Tango, The Dance of Design
Feng Shui and the Tango, The Essential Chapters
25th Anniversary Edition
FS&T Prosperity Lessons
FS&T Happiness Lessons
The Dream Desk Quiz
Creating Clarity

About the Authors, the Books, & Amicis Winery Tours

Ralph and Lahni DeAmicis found their way into writing tour and travel books by starting to create a book about winery buildings for their series on Feng Shui, but the research was going excruciatingly slow. While the winery staff knew the wines, they rarely knew about the buildings. Then one day, while coming out of the Stag's Leap Wine Cellars, Ralph chatted up a local limousine driver who was a wealth of information about interesting winery buildings, apparently that knowledge was part of a tour guide's toolbox.

Seeing a research opportunity that would also put some money in their pockets, Ralph got a part time job driving tours, coming home daily with notes and photographs of the wineries. As he navigated his way around the various valleys, they realized that even though the wineries are the biggest attraction, there wasn't a good 'winery' tour book. So, their project about winery buildings morphed into their first guidebook in 2008, becoming the first in a series of updates and improvements.

After two years of touring for other companies Ralph & Lahni decided to start their own tour company, Amicis Tours, to make the continuing research easier. They soon realized that it's a fun business that brings them to beautiful places while connecting them to the winemaking community and visitors from around the world, they are both multi-lingual. In 2012 they started producing the TV show 'Wine Country at Work' which allowed them to more deeply explore topics that they found interesting. In 2022 the show was rebranded as Wine Country in Shorts, in alignment with their new book of short stories about the North Bay region.

In 2023 they added a new book, The 2023 Wine Tasting Calendar, that uses the position of the Moon to provide guidance about to manage a wine tasting. The 2024 edition is out and 2025 is underway. Enjoy, and travel safely and happily!

Find their books and videos at:
www.AmicisTours.com

Cuore Libre Publishing Books and Calendars

From the Back Cover of

Wine Country in Shorts
The Stories of Napa and Sonoma
by Ralph & Lahni DeAmicis

Sonoma and Napa are the northern most points in the Spanish Empire's expansion in the Americas. We're convinced that they came to these beautiful valleys and thought, "We've arrived in Eden, we don't need to go any farther." It is a special place, that at one time was considered the far ends of the Earth, a place where explorers, adventurers and the foolish went, which made for a very interesting demographic.

What is surprising is how different Sonoma and Napa are, located on either side of the Mayacamas Mountains. We often describe Sonoma as the older sister, who is a good-looking girl, a great cook and gardener, always content with her family and friends. Napa is her golden-haired little brother, who is endlessly curious about the outside world, and every time he walks in the room, everybody makes a fuss. It drives Sonoma crazy, but Napa adores his big sister.

These stories and insights about Wine Country, covering its origins and culture, were gathered over twenty years, while we stood in the back of tasting rooms listening to hosts talk about the region, while pouring wine for our tour clients. We found that every story had at least three versions, so we've melded them together, using as our guide what felt right. They present a wonderfully revealing picture of this remarkable place and the people who have helped make it special. We hope you enjoy them.

**To find our other titles
Visit WineCountryInShorts.com**

www.ingramcontent.com/pod-product-compliance
Lightning Source LLC
LaVergne TN
LVHW012028060526
838201LV00061B/4511